CAUSE OF DEATH:
A Writer's Guide to Death, Murder and Forensic Medicine

by
Keith D. Wilson, M.D.

Writer's Digest Books

Cincinnati, Ohio

Cause of Death: A Writer's Guide to Death, Murder and Forensic Medicine. Copyright © 1992 by Keith D. Wilson. Printed and bound in the United States of America. All rights reserved. No part of this book may be reproduced in any form or by any electronic or mechanical means including information storage and retrieval systems without permission in writing from the publisher, except by a reviewer, who may quote brief passages in a review. Published by Writer's Digest Books, an imprint of F&W Publications, Inc., 1507 Dana Avenue, Cincinnati, Ohio 45207. 1-800-289-0963. First edition.

96   95   94   93   5   4   3   2

Library of Congress Cataloging-in-Publication Data

Wilson, Keith
   Cause of death : a writer's guide to death, murder and forensic medicine /
Keith Wilson.
      p.   cm.
   Includes bibliographical references and index.
   ISBN 0-89879-524-9
   1. Medical jurisprudence. 2. Death in literature. I. Title.
RA1051.W62   1992
614'.1'0248 — dc20   92-15729
                                             CIP

Edited by Charles Clark
Cover illustration by Chris Spollen

About the Author

Dr. Keith Wilson is a graduate of Ohio State University School of Medicine, where he earned several academic honors and graduated cum laude. Following medical school, he completed his residency in Denver, Colorado.

He is currently the director of the Magnetic Resonance Imaging Section at the Toledo Hospital.

His first novel, Life Form, *a medical thriller, was published by the Putnam-Berkley Publishing Group.*

His short story, "The Cottonwood," was a finalist, winning honorable mention, in the Hemingway Short Story contest.

He lives in Toledo, Ohio, and is currently at work on his third book.

Acknowledgments

First, a special thanks to my dear friend and greatest teacher, Gary Provost, for his ideas, enthusiasm and encouragement.

To Dr. George Magill, FACEP, Assistant Medical Director of the Emergency Department, Magruder Hospital.

To Dr. Diane M. Scala-Barnett, Deputy Coroner and Forensic Pathologist for Lucas County and Clinical Assistant Professor of Pathology at the Medical College of Ohio, for her kind assistance and direction.

To Charles Clark for his professional editing, patience, and knowledge, to see this project to its completion.

To Ann Higgins for her generous work and guidance.

And to my dear wife Cathy for her support, patience and invaluable suggestions that allowed this book to happen.

Dedicated to Robert Leighton Strong

Foreword

In 1974 I wrote a novel called *The Pie in The Face Murders*, in which I needed to murder two characters by having each one smacked in the face with a pie. That book was never published, for a variety of reasons, not the least of which was the fact that the deadly pie I invented was so cumbersome and complicated that it quickly revealed that most unwelcome figure in the novel, the writer at work. This pie of mine contained filed-down baseball cleats, ground glass, a plastic wrapper, and enough poison to wipe out half of Kansas. It was supposed to be taken for an ordinary pie in the plot, but in fact this pie would have weighed enough to alarm even the most naive pie-eater. Clearly, I had no idea of what I was doing. If I had had Keith Wilson's book *Cause of Death* at the time, maybe things would have been different. Maybe my assassin would have been able to bake a pie that was simple and believable, and able to cause death within the time span that I required.

That is just one example of a time in my career when this book would have been useful. Overall, I have killed relatively few people in stories, compared to, say a mystery writer. Several of my books have been for children, several have been for writers, and several have been true stories. But even at that, I have found it necessary to give one lovable old man a terminal illness; I've had to arrange murders that looked like accidents for a couple of young women; and, as a true-crime writer, I've had to describe the moment of death for several real-life victims. In other words, I have needed Wilson's book for years, and what I formerly accomplished through a series of time-consuming phone calls and interviews, I will now accomplish by thumbing through *Cause of Death*.

After love, death is certainly the number-one subject of fiction. Mysteries, crime stories, war stories, true crimes, generational sagas and historical novels, to name just a few, all require death to move their plots forward.

The importance of death to fiction can be summed up in two words: *conflict* and *stakes*. Fiction is about conflict and death is the most chilling and lasting result of conflict. And fiction cannot work without high stakes. The highest stakes of all are life and death. Imagine reading a mystery in which the victim is simply wounded. Imagine reading a *Gone With the Wind*, in which the Civil War claims no lives. Imagine reading *A Christmas Carol*, in which Scrooge is told to shape up or he will earn 20 percent less money next year. Remove death from most stories and what you have is a cure for insomnia.

So it is required of any writer that he or she deal with death often and accurately. Until now we have had little to go on but our own rare and subjective experiences with death, and the descriptions of other writers. But now, with *Cause of Death*, we have something we have all dreamed of — an expert at death by our side as we write. Keith Wilson, in addition to being a highly respected doctor, is a fine novelist. This is a relief, for nothing could be deadlier to your writing than a dry description of death from the pen of a pedantic physician. Wilson writes here clearly, vividly and with great enthusiasm for his subject. He speaks not to medical students, but to writers.

In this book you will discover not just how to make characters die, but how to do it with flair, creativity and credibility, in a manner that is both compelling and accurate. You want to knock somebody off and make it look like an accident? Wilson tells you how. You want to give a character six months to get his affairs in order, and then put him six feet under? Wilson tells you how. You want to make a murder of one character so horrendous that another character cannot resist arranging something even more bizarre? You want someone to die peacefully in his sleep? You want to execute a prisoner, poison a blackmailer, garotte a guard, certify a death, or save someone's life in the emergency room? In the pages of this book, Dr. Wilson tells you how to do all of these things. And a lot more.

For me, *Cause of Death* will be added to those books that I keep within arm's reach of my keyboard, and I advise that you give the book a similar place of honor. This is a book on death that will make all writers' lives easier, and certainly, it will help this writer to bake a pie you could die for.

Gary Provost

Introduction: The Role of Death In Literature

Life and death are in constant conflict; one cannot occur without the other. To experience life we must also taste death. This eternal conflict and interdependence is a recurring theme in books, movies, plays and operas.

Because death is an inescapable reality of life, as a writer, you must deal with it, weaving it into your story, either as a secondary player, or as the major theme.

To write believably, you cannot avoid conflict, arguments, fights, riots or war. Conflict is the driving force behind all plots and must be met straight-on. Death is life's ultimate conflict; the eternal human struggle to understand, cope with, and finally accept and make peace with it. Your characters must be at war with death: screaming out with pain when it robs them of their children; horrified when they face their own death; and fearful when they ponder its meaning.

Some popular books and movies where death plays a major role in the story include: *Gone With the Wind, Hamlet, The Great Gatsby, Of Mice and Men, Steel Magnolias, Love Story, Dying Young, Terms of Endearment, The Devil's Advocate, Our Town, Dark Victory* and *Beaches*.

Even in comedy, one cannot escape the tragedy of death. In the movie *City Slickers*, three best friends struggle with the meaning of life and death. Curly, the trail boss (played by Jack Palance), holds up one finger and says, "Only one thing in life really matters. You stick to that and everything else don't mean shit!" Curly dies, but life renews when Billy Crystal helps to deliver a calf named Norman. As a result, the story changes, and brings about the characters' growth.

Mysteries, thrillers and, more recently, the true-crime story, are big-selling genres that continue to gain popularity. What is the allure that draws millions of readers into the world of murder?

Death is the final mystery, the last unknown; our fear of death intrigues us. Gary Provost, a well-known true-crime writer of such books as *Without Mercy, Across the Border* and *How to Write and Sell True Crime*, says, "Of all the crimes that could be perpetrated on us, we fear murder the most. It is our own primeval fear of death that draws us in and makes us fascinated with murder."

Cause of Death is a practical information book targeted specifically to writers and their needs. It is intended to be a writer's medical and legal guide to death and murder. It covers forensic medicine, emergency room procedures, accurate medical terminology, and judicial executions.

This book discusses natural and unnatural causes of death; murder and suicides; the autopsy; the coroner's report; what happens to the evidence, and how the body is handled. *Cause of Death* is focused to your specific needs as a writer and covers a wide range of information that will help you with specific details for appropriate scenes. However, because of the obvious limitation of the length and scope of this book, you may need more information than provided here. There are complete textbooks that cover in detail any one of these subjects that may be a major theme in your story, and an extensive reference list is included at the end of this book to direct to you to a specific source.

There is a glossary in this book providing explanations of medical terminology and procedures. Words defined in the glossary appear in boldface type the first time they are used.

I have included excerpts by other authors to show how they handled the subject matter. How much detail or specific terminology should be used? Authors handle the material in their own style, but all of them use accurate, specific details. How much to use is part of the art of writing, and that is something you will have to decide for yourself.

Cause of Death is divided into three parts to organize the material in a way to help writers both understand and utilize death as a vital part of their story.

Part I defines what constitutes death and details the dying process. The medical and legal criteria for defining death are outlined.

Part II goes from the general to the specific and is a "how-to" section for writers. This section describes what happens to a person (or character from your story) from specific injuries to medical treatment in the emergency room to autopsy and finally, to burial. Capital punishment is also covered. The information in Part II should enable you to write a factual hospital scene, describe an autopsy or use medical-police procedures accurately.

Part III discusses the theme of death and is a general review of death in literature. This section shows how death plays a vital role in fiction, plays, movies and operas. Death itself is discussed, followed by a detailed review of accidental deaths, sudden deaths from natural causes, and deaths from chronic illnesses. This section shows the importance of death, and gives varied examples of how other authors handled it. Finally, the moral, ethical and political issues relating to death are examined.

Table of Contents

Part I
DEATH AND DYING

1 Death 2
Defining the terms death *and* dying.
Definition of Death
Death and the Dying Process
The Terminal State

Part II
MEDICAL AND LEGAL PROCEDURES RELATED TO DEATH

2 Emergency! 10
How emergency rooms work.
ER Procedures, Terminology, Equipment
Evaluation of the Patient and Vital Signs
CPR and Resuscitation
Blood Loss and Shock
Trauma to Head, Chest, Abdomen
Reportable Cases of Rape, Child Abuse, DOA

3 Declared Dead 46
The process of pronouncing death.
Legal Time of Death
Who Declares a Person Dead?
How Is It Carried Out?
Where Is the Procedure Done?
What Criteria Is Used?
The Death Certificate
  Who Fills It Out?
  Where Does It Go?
  What Information Is Included?
  Fetal Death and Death Certificate
  Sample Form

4 How the Body Is Handled *52*

Who handles the body, how they do it, and why they do it that way.

    What Happens to the Body After Death Is Discovered
    Religious Beliefs and Customs
    Laws Regarding Burial and Disposal of the Body
    Cremation, Embalming and Burial
    Morgue and Funeral Home
    Funeral Director and Mortician
    The Coroner and Medical Examiner
    What Constitutes a Coroner's Case

5 Time of Death *62*

How to determine the time of death by analyzing the body's condition.

    Determination of Time of Death
    Postmortem Changes of the Body
    Rigor Mortis and Lividity

6 The Autopsy *69*

How medical investigators establish the cause of death.

    Which Cases Get Autopsied
    Reportable Deaths
    Inside the Morgue
    Autopsy Description
    Medical Evidence
    Photography of Body
    Toxicology
    Identification of Body-Remains
    Autopsy of Fetus and Newborn Infant

7 Murder or Suicide? *94*

Deciding the manner and mechanism of death.

    The Killer Instinct
    Suicide
    Shooting
    Drowning
    Asphyxiation by Hanging, Strangulation
    Poisoning
    Stabbing

8 **Crime and Punishment**   *123*

Where and how capital punishment is performed.
>History of Executions
>Public Executions
>State-by-State Laws and Methods
>Hanging
>Firing Squad
>Electric Chair
>Gas Chamber
>Lethal Injection

Part III
CAUSES OF DEATH

9 **Accidents**   *142*

Ways in which deaths occur.
>Accidents in Literature
>Death From Nature (Animals, Insects, Mushrooms)
>Falling (Stairs, Ladder, Roof, Bathtub, Shower)
>Choking
>Death on the Farm
>Electrocution
>Lightning
>Death Among Children
>Emergency Medical Services

10 **Sudden Death**   *167*

A discussion of death from natural causes.
>Sudden Death in Literature
>Sudden Death Defined
>Cardiac Causes and Heart Attack
>Worked to Death
>Stroke

11 **Chronic Illness and Disease**   *174*

Debilitating diseases and the process of slow death.
>Review of Chronic Illness in Literature
>Plagues and Scourges: Tuberculosis, Cholera, AIDS
>Brain Injury and Disability

12 Controversies Involving Death   *185*

A brief look at moral, ethical and political issues associated with death.

    Emotionally Induced Death and Voodoo
    Cryonics
    Hospice
    Right to Die and Euthanasia
    Living Wills

Glossary   *197*

Bibliography   *202*

Index   *203*

PART I

DEATH AND DYING

O N E

DEATH

Joe Burlington slithered cautiously to the edge of the hole in the ice, holding the rope attached to the diver. Something broke the surface of the black water. Burlington reached down into the icy darkness and grabbed the arm of the little boy.

The lifeless body resisted Burlington's attempts to pull it from the water, but he held on relentlessly with fingers numbed by the frigid water, refusing to let go. After finally getting him onto the ice, Burlington pulled the boy away from the hole and carried him to shore where others waited.

Paramedics rushed to administer aid. They rolled the boy onto his back. His skin was a dark gray-blue color and his face was expressionless, eyes half-open and glazed. "No pulse," one of them said. Five paramedics trained for just such an emergency moved in unison to revive the little boy: They started an I.V., wrapped him in a warm blanket, gave him oxygen and then administered CPR. Burlington glanced at his watch; the boy had been under the ice at least thirty-five minutes.

His mother looked down at him and screamed. "Oh, my God! He's dead."

Clinically dead, Burlington thought, but he's not gone yet. With luck, the little boy might be sledding again next year with his friends.

DEFINITION OF DEATH

Dead: Having ceased to live; lifeless.

Death: The permanent cessation of all vital functions in an animal.

That's the *American Heritage Dictionary*'s definition. The California District Court of Appeals stated in a 1950 ruling: *Death occurs precisely when life ceases and does not occur until the heart stops beating and respiration ends.* That was the standard definition for years, relating to heart activity and respiration.

But with the advent of organ transplants, the legal system is becoming more involved in the field of medicine and the courts are deciding when life-support systems can be turned off. Ethical and legal questions have created a newer definition. Because of techniques used in **CPR** that can restore cardiac activity and breathing, the current medical-legal definition relates to the viability of the brain.

Today, the absence of pulse and breathing is called **clinical death** and was the condition of the boy who fell through the ice. But clinical death is a reversible process.

Both the medical and legal professions have recognized and designated **brain death** as the most meaningful indicator of human death because the viability of the brain defines human life.

The Current Medical-Legal Definition of Death

Death has occurred when all cerebral function has ceased and is irreversible.

The following conditions must exist before someone is taken off mechanical support or before their body can be harvested for organ donation:

Medical-Legal Criteria for Determining Brain Death

- Bilateral dilation and fixation of pupils
- Absence of all reflexes
- Cessation of respiration (breathing) without assistance
- Cessation of cardiac action
- Completely flat brain wave tracing

The process of brain death follows this sequence, beginning first with the dilation and fixation of pupils and ultimately ending in a completely flat brain wave tracing. All five criteria must be present before a person may be declared dead and taken off mechanical support.

Death and the Dying Process

It hath often been said that it is not death, but dying, which is terrible.

Henry Fielding, *Amelia*, 1745

Death is not a continuous process; rather, it is a fixed event that takes place at a precise time. Death is that moment in time when the brain has no life or function left. But dying, the process of getting to that moment of death, occurs over seconds, minutes or hours. It is a course of events that will result in death.

In many respects, death and dying are similar to birth. The process of being born takes minutes or hours (contraction of the uterus with labor pains, movement through the birth canal in slow, twisting stages until, finally, the moment of birth). Birth itself is an exact moment in time and is listed on the birth certificate down to the second. Similarly, a specific time is also recorded on a death certificate (if the time of death was witnessed), indicating the exact moment death occurs.

The process of dying, like being born, usually occurs over a course of time. However, unlike birth, there is more than one way dying can occur:

- Instantaneous death (without the dying process)
- Acute dying

- Dying in shock
- Progressive dying (can include dying from "natural causes" as well as death from disease)

The difference between these deaths is the duration of the dying process. Instantaneous death means that within a split second a person goes from being alive to complete death without going through any dying sequence. This follows events such as an explosion or a high-velocity impact. For example, an airplane crash resulting in total fragmentation of the body.

Acute dying involves a very short progression of events. The dying process will take seconds or a few minutes when it is the result of a gunshot injury, a massive heart attack with **ventricular fibrillation** or a fatal impact such as falling from a great distance or being in an auto accident. Even if both heart activity and respiration stop instantly (and the body is intact), it takes seconds or minutes for brain death to follow.

The statement "He died instantly" is usually incorrect. We console ourselves that a victim did not suffer, which is probably true, but the moment of death did not occur instantly; it followed a very short dying process.

Dying in **shock** takes even longer, because there is time for other factors to come into play. Shock results from inadequate perfusion of blood to meet organ needs. Shock can result from lack of blood (loss with massive hemorrhage) or from ineffective heart pumping (heart failure, heart attack), both of which cause low blood pressure and inadequate circulation of blood.

Shock, if not reversed, either by replacing blood through transfusion or by causing the heart to pump effectively, will lead to a vicious cycle of lethal multiple organ failure until death occurs.

Progressive dying takes minutes or hours and the person may be conscious for most of the dying process. Sometimes the person will utter final words, or give a final gesture before slipping into death. A mother may call her children in and say farewell.

How do people know they are, at that moment, dying; that the words they utter will be their final words?

We don't know the exact answer to that, but maybe the dying person is aware of the changes in his or her body, as organ systems fail in sequence like lights going out in a city in large sections, until finally there is darkness.

The Terminal State

The terminal stages of life, in both rapid and protracted dying, are followed by panorganic death, i.e., irreversible overall tissue destruction. This is a slow process ranging from five minutes required for brain cells to suffer irreversible damage, to about thirty minutes for the heart muscle to cease electrical activity and stop beating.

The sequence of events during the terminal stages of dying depends to some degree on the cause. If a person chokes and cannot breathe, the heart will continue beating for several minutes, long after the person has lost consciousness due to brain **anoxia**. But if the person suffers a fatal heart attack and the heart stops beating (**asystole**), breathing will continue for a period of time. With massive blood loss and hemorrhaging, first there is loss of consciousness due to lack of perfusion of the brain, then the heart activity ceases. Finally, breathing stops.

However, the usual sequence during the terminal state includes the following:

1. *Sequential loss.* First there is loss of mentation (person disoriented and confused), followed by loss of consciousness, then loss of circulation as the heart stops and normal breathing slows down.

2. *Terminal apnea.* Normal rhythmical breathing stops.

3. *Agonal state.* The period of time after onset of pulselessness (absence of circulation) and after terminal **apnea**; there are gasping respirations and gurgling (death rattle).

4. *Clinical death.* Coma, apnea and no gasping, no pulse, but brain failure is still reversible at this point. Immediate CPR with restoration of circulation and air flow must happen here to prevent rapid dying and breakdown of brain cells.

   With clinical death, the person is unconscious, has no heartbeat and is not breathing. But clinical death is a transition between life and death. If clinical death is not immediately reversed, the person will rapidly progress to brain death — which is *not* reversible.

5. *Vegetative state.* If circulation is delayed further beyond the phase of clinical death, there can be continued **coma** with an abnormal EEG resulting in the vegetative state. This is not a normal part of dying; it occurs only when there has been

intervention to prevent the progression of further brain damage and death.

6. *Brain death.* If circulation to the brain is further impaired, the result is deep coma, apnea with no respiration, and no EEG activity (brain dead). At this phase, the entire brain is irreversibly silenced.

Summary of the Terminal Dying Sequence

1. Unconsciousness
2. Apnea (no breathing) or gasping respirations
3. Pulselessness of carotid or femoral arteries
4. Death-like appearance (cyanotic-blue appearance, pupils dull, fixed and dilated)

With modern medical technology it is possible to keep the heart beating (by means of various pumping devices or electrical **pacemakers**); to maintain breathing (by respirator); to continue feeding (by intravenous infusion of fluids and electrolytes); and to remove waste material (by dialysis); and still be legally dead. To be legally dead, a person must be brain dead, with no EEG activity of the brain, no cornea sensitivity, no pupil reaction to light, no cough reflex and no spontaneous breathing.

I'm not afraid to die. I just don't want to be there when it happens.

— Woody Allen

Nobody looks forward to death. In fact, we tend to ignore the inevitability of death. But when we do think about our own death, we allow ourselves to hope that when we die we'll just drop dead in our tracks, with no extended pain or heroic efforts with tubes, I.V.'s or mechanical ventilators. Just jump from being alive and well, to flat-out dead.

Many people may fantasize of dying in their own home, peaceful and comfortable, with those people they love best around them. Gently, without pain, they breathe their last breath.

But we do not choose death; it chooses us, coming like a thief in the night. Unexpected and uninvited.

Because I could not stop for Death,
He kindly stopped for me.

Emily Dickinson

PART II

MEDICAL AND LEGAL PROCEDURES RELATED TO DEATH

T W O

EMERGENCY!

Dan's Convenience Store
10:45 P.M.
Friday Night

Bobby Hicks glanced up at the clock again. Only fifteen more minutes until he could close. He'd calculated on scrap paper for the tenth time how much he needed: two more months and he'd have enough to buy a car. Then he would quit this ridiculous job and try out for the varsity baseball team. Catcher was the only position he'd even consider, to be like Johnny Bench, squatting down behind home plate, crouched between the ump and batter; the smell of rosin on wood in his face, while he fingered the next pitch to the mound.

Two girls came in and rummaged around the shelves for gum and cigarettes. Bobby glanced at them then turned his attention back to cleaning the coffee machine. When they came to the counter he saw that they were both average looking—a six on the Bobby scale—but the tall one had a great figure.

Seeing them reminded him of why he needed a car, and soon. He had needs that a bicycle couldn't fulfill.

As they left, a man whisked past them and went to the magazine section. Bobby pulled out the receipt box and was ready to close out the register. He lifted the cash drawer and took the larger bills that were kept underneath, then closed the register while he counted. There were four payroll checks that he had cashed for customers, three fifties and a single hundred. All the small bills—ones, tens and twenties—were in the cash drawer.

Bobby, intent on counting the cash, became aware of a presence and looked up to see the man standing inches from his face, a huge chrome-plated "Dirty Harry" revolver in his hand.

"Open the register. Move it!" He waved the gun at the register, while glancing nervously at the parking lot. Bobby, not sure of what he had heard, turned toward the man again, an act that angered the nervous gunman. He slammed the butt of the gun into the side of Bobby's head. "Open the goddamned register!"

Blood streamed down Bobby's face as he staggered backward from the blow, then reached for the register and opened it. The man started stuffing money into his pocket. Bobby stepped back and put his hand to his head. The pain was blinding.

The man jammed the last fistful of bills into his pocket and nervously looked outside again. Suddenly and without warning, he held the gun at arm's length, aimed point-blank at Bobby's chest and fired.

The gun kicked with a huge explosion and the impact threw Bobby against the wall. A crushing pressure caved in on his sternum like a giant hand, and he opened his mouth to breathe, trying to will air into a lung that had been ripped by a slug, a collapsed lung that was now filling with blood instead of air. He gasped for breath and coughed up pink froth, then crumpled to the floor.

An unrelenting, bone-numbing cold gripped him; his hands started twitching, then his whole body shook uncontrollably; the heels of his Nikes tapped a faint staccato on the floor. His own heartbeat drummed in his ears as a fearful darkness swept over him.

The EMS paramedics had already called ahead to the Memorial Hospital Emergency Room, and the ER staff was waiting. The pneumatic doors flew open and Bobby Hicks was whisked into Trauma Room One. Blood soaked his shirt, ran from the corners of his mouth and streamed from his forehead. Each labored cough sprayed more blood from his mouth.

"This boy has massive blood loss," one of the paramedics called out, wiping blood from his face with the back of his hand. Droplets of Bobby's blood splattered the paramedic's glasses, his face and the entire front of his shirt.

That night, Bobby Hicks became a case of "penetrating trauma"—a term used in the shock-trauma unit of the ER. The shock-trauma team moved into position around him, with knives, forceps, scissors, needles, sponges, tubes and catheters all laid out and within easy reach.

Six people swarmed over him, a dozen hands working in unison to stabilize him. Blood was drawn from a vessel in Bobby's groin, one of the bigger vessels that remain functional even when blood pressure drops and small vessels collapse. A nurse threaded a catheter up his urethra and into his bladder. Electrical leads attached to circular patches were taped to his chest; a blood-pressure cuff was wrapped around his arm and inflated.

Dr. Tom Parks, the senior ER resident, quickly placed his stethoscope on Bobby's chest. He looked up as Bobby coughed up more blood. "Suction," he ordered. A nurse handed him a plastic tube and turned on the suction. Parks fed the suction tube to the back of Bobby's throat, sucking back pink foam and red blood. "Let's intubate him."

A nurse placed a tray on the table and peeled off the sterile cover, exposing the instruments. With Bobby's neck extended, Parks guided a breathing tube down his throat and positioned a polystyrene endotracheal tube into the trachea. A respiratory therapist attached an Ambu bag and started to ventilate him manually by forcing air into his lungs.

"Hang a liter of Ringers and dextran," Parks said. "And order two units of O-negative stat. What's his blood pressure?"

"Sixty. Pulse 120," one of the nurses answered. A unit of O-negative was already being started, with a pressure cuff inflated around the bag to force blood rapidly through the tubing. "Pressure fifty."

His blood pressure was in free-fall. He was leaking blood from somewhere, lots of it. "Type and cross match for another six units,"

Parks said. He noticed the gash over Bobby's right ear and wiped the blood away with a four-inch gauze pad. He snapped on a pair of sterile gloves and his fingers probed the skull under the cut. He felt a sickening crunch as bone gave way and his finger sank into a mushy depression. He snapped on his penlight and checked Bobby's pupils. "Depressed skull fracture . . . pinpoint right pupil. Order an emergency CT scan and get a neurosurgeon down here!"

Parks turned his attention from the head to the chest. One of the nurses cut away Bobby's blood-soaked shirt with a pair of large bandage-scissors. A dark sea of blood flowed from a black hole just to the left of his sternum, and with each labored breath, bloody foam gurgled out from the bullet wound.

"Christ, he's got a sucking chest wound," Parks said. After moving his stethoscope across Bobby's chest, he said, "No breath sounds on this side. Pneumothorax. Get a chest tube for me."

His fingers probed for the superior edge of the fifth rib, along the mid-axillary line directly below the armpit. He scrubbed the area with Betadine antiseptic and, using a scalpel, quickly made a one-inch long incision, then poked his finger into the bleeding hole to widen it by blunt dissection of the tissues. He fed the trochar over the top of the rib and into the chest cavity, then pulled it out and advanced the chest tube. He was reassured by the fogging of the clear plastic tube as air from Bobby's chest moved in and out with each breath. Parks attached the chest tube to a suction bottle, but he was concerned at the cyanotic color of the boy. He knew the blood gases were lousy, but right now he didn't know what else to do.

"Bring the portable machine over here and get a chest X ray now."

Before the X ray could be taken, the ECG monitor's shrill alarm sounded. The tracing showed a straight line.

"Asystole," a nurse called out, then started resuscitation by pumping the sternum while the respiratory therapist continued ventilating him by squeezing the Ambu bag.

"Call a code!" Parks bellowed out.

The hospital paging system came to life in seconds: "CODE-99, Shock-trauma unit. CODE-99, Shock-trauma unit."

The X-ray technologist pushed the portable machine out of the way as the crash-cart was moved over. A surgeon, pharmacist, anesthesiologist and two more nurses from the code-team burst into the room and moved into action. Parks grabbed the electric defibrillator paddles and pressed them against the left side of Bobby's chest.

"Everybody clear!"

The staff stepped away from him and a quick jolt made Bobby's body jerk involuntarily. The tracing on the monitor was still flat.

"Again!" But the results were the same.

"Piggyback a bottle of high-dose epinephrine, and titrate," Parks called out, "and push another amp of sodium bicarb." The pharmacist injected 10 mg of epinephrine into a 100 cc bottle then hung it up to run piggyback with the dextran tubing. The ER nurse continued cardiac compression.

Parks and the code team attempted electrical conversion six more times, but Bobby's heart refused to beat. The tracing line was flat; his heart remained still. Parks turned to the surgeon to determine what to do next.

If they had to, the surgical team could crack a chest inside of three minutes using little more than a knife and a rib spreader. After shoving the pale-pink lung aside, the stalled heart would be exposed. Sometimes squeezing the lifeless organ by hand could successfully jump start it; with luck, the injured person would survive. Now the surgeon would have to make that decision.

The surgeon turned on his penlight and directed its light directly into Bobby's eyes. Dull, unblinking eyes stared back at him with large black pupils. It had been forty minutes since they started; now it was over. "Pupils are fixed and dilated. I see no reason to crack the chest. Cancel the code."

Everybody stopped, stood there a moment, then went about their business of preparing Bobby Hicks for the morgue, calling the coroner's office and the police, cleaning up the room, and getting ready for the next case to come crashing through the door.

It was Friday night, and they didn't know how many more trauma cases they would see before the night was over.

The Emergency Room and Treatment of a Critical Patient

It is impossible to cover in this book the hundreds of different types of emergencies that are seen daily in any emergency room. I wrote the previous scene to show writers how to incorporate medical terms, equipment and emergency procedures into their stories.

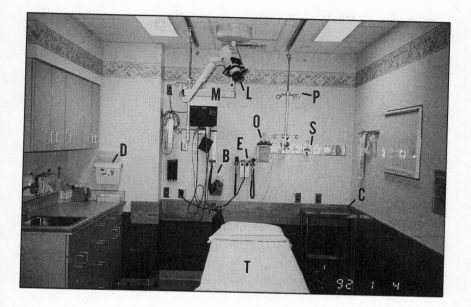

Emergency Room standard treatment room.

T—Treatment table
X—X-ray view box
L—Overhead spotlight
P—Overhead suspended I.V. pole
M—Monitor for ECG heart activity
D—Disposal for biohazardous materials (needles, tubing)
S—Wall-mounted suction
O—Wall-mounted oxygen
B—Blood pressure cuff and gauge
E—ENT otoscope and ophthalmoscope for ears, nose, throat evaluation
C—Utility cart (for holding dressings, instruments, surgical trays)

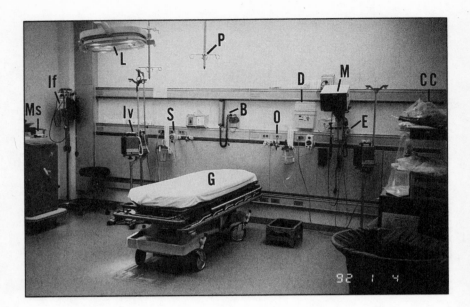

Emergency Room set up to handle major shock-trauma.

- G – Gurney cart
- B – Blood pressure cuff and gauge
- O – Oxygen
- S – Suction
- M – Monitor for electrocardiogram
- E – ENT otoscope and ophthalmoscope for ears, nose, throat exams
- CC – Crash cart, containing drugs, oral airway, tubing, needles
- D – Disposal for used needles, syringes and tubing
- Ms – Medical supplies
- L – Overhead surgical lamp
- P – Overhead suspended I.V. pole
- If – I.V. infusion pumps for administering I.V. fluids or blood rapidly
- Iv – I.V. electrical infusion pump

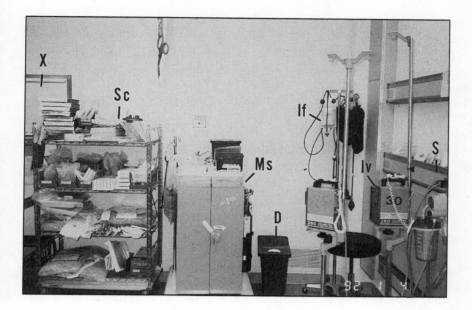

Emergency Room set up to handle major shock-trauma.

    X — X-ray view box
    Sc — Supply cart, with cut-down trays, minor surgery trays, sterile dressings, bandages,
        I.V. fluids
    Ms — Medical supply cabinet
    D — Disposal for biohazardous materials (needles, tubing)
    If — Infusion pumps for administering blood rapidly to treat shock
    Iv — Intravenous infusion pumps
    S — Wall-mounted suction

An important word of caution: a few, well-chosen medical terms will add depth and realism to your writing. But trying to use too many details or phrases will kill the scene along with the victim. The story is what is important to the reader, not a litany of medical terms. Sprinkle technical terms into your story like spices, adding just a bit here and there for flavor.

Bobby Hicks's case was detailed here to describe for you how a typical **code** is handled (cardiac arrest and resuscitation) and to show how the police become involved after a gunshot injury. Using this chapter, you will be able to write an emergency room scene that is both exciting and realistic.

The modern emergency room is the gathering place for the sick, dying and injured. More than ninety million people visit emergency rooms in the United States each year. The medical ER staff works long hours, sorting through the ailing bodies, wounded spirits and disordered lives, attending to the injuries, diseases and deaths that stalk the streets of our cities. Although overburdened, understaffed and glutted with patients, emergency rooms have become the primary source of medical care for the poor.

Everyday the ER staff fights a war: to treat stabbings, heart attacks, rapes, drug overdoses, mangled bodies from the highways, the depressed and despondent, and, on a happier note, deliveries. They battle their own stress and strain from overcrowding, tense periods of life-threatening crises, and the ever-present personal risks of AIDS, hepatitis and tuberculosis.

Triage of the Patient

Triage is a French word meaning "to sort." A new patient is triaged to determine what is the most critical treatment priority. Drug overdoses, acute heart attacks, fractured femurs and miscarriages with hemorrhage must all be first sorted out and identified, then prioritized as to the critical extent of the patient's problem. This process is called triaging.

System Priorities

Basic
- Life
- Limb
- Function

- Cosmetic

Highest Priority
- Respiratory
- Cardiovascular
- Hemorrhage (blood loss)

Very High Priority
- Shock
- Intra-abdominal bleeding

High Priority
- Head/spine injury
- Burns

Low Priority
- Cuts
- Fractures

When a patient is brought to the ER with any significant degree of injury, the initial exam is to see:

- If the patient is breathing
- That there is a good heart rate (the heart is working to circulate the blood to vital organs)
- That there is good blood pressure (there is in fact sufficient volume of blood for the heart to pump)

These are the ABCs: Airway, Breathing, Circulation. All three factors are immediately crucial to sustaining life and must be correlated before any other injury can be considered and dealt with. The measurements of these (heart rate, blood pressure, rate of respiration and temperature) are called, collectively, the **vital signs**.

The 60-Second Examination

Action	Abnormality	Cause	Reaction
Observe respiratory effort	Stridor	Upper airway obstruction	Clear airway Intubate when needed
	Tachypnea	Pneumothorax	Provide oxygen; obtain ABC chest film

Action	Abnormality	Cause	Reaction
		Pulmonary parenchymal damage Acidosis, hypoxia	Give fluids and insert chest tube when indicated
Touch skin	Diaphoresis	Environmental exposure	Recheck core temp., BP
	Cold Vasoconstriction	Shock	Provide fluid support, correct temp.
Palpate head	Hematomas of scalp	Contusions Underlying fractures	Assess neurologic status
Palpate neck	Tenderness	Cervical strain	Stabilize neck
		Cervical fracture	Obtain C-spine films
Palpate trachea	Shift from midline	Pneumothorax	Insert chest tube
Palpate chest and listen to breath sounds	Subcutaneous air Decreased breath sounds	Possible pneumothorax	Obtain chest film Insert chest tube
Listen to heart sounds	Muffled sound	Possible cardiac tamponade	Perform ECG, recheck blood pressure Give fluids Perform pericardiocentesis
Palpate abdomen	Tenderness	Intra-abdominal blood	Consider peritoneal lavage Determine Hct-baseline, recheck orthostatics
Observe genitals	Blood from urethral meatus	Urethral disruption	Consider retrograde urethrogram
Palpate pelvis	Tenderness	Pelvic fracture	Consider concomitant pathology
	Instability		Obtain pelvic film; perform urinalysis

Action	Abnormality	Cause	Reaction
Palpate extremities	Tenderness	Fracture	Immobilize patient
Question patient	Inappropriate response	CNS, injury	Obtain skull films
		Shock	Perform CT scan, burr holes, red BP

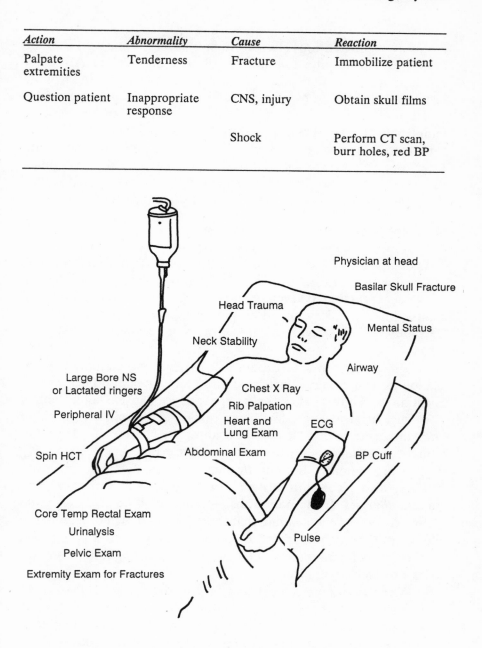

Notice how the fictitious ER staff in my opening scene with Bobby's arrival at the hospital followed rigidly the protocol of ABCs for life support. First, they determined that Bobby was having trouble breathing because of bleeding into his chest, so they suctioned his throat to clear out any debris or clots, then **intubated** him with an **endotracheal** tube. Then, they ran O-negative blood and dextran rapidly to replace blood loss and sustain blood pressure. Blood and fluids were forced in rapidly through large bore needles (18-gauge or larger). After the ER staff attended to the necessary ABCs, they did a thorough head-to-toe examination to assess other injuries.

General Appearance of the Patient

A quick analysis of the appearance of the patient can tell the physician a lot of information. If the patient is cold and clammy, covered with beads of sweat and has a gray pallor, this is usually a **vaso-vagal reaction** to severe pain (heart attack, kidney stone, labor pains), internal injury, blood loss or fear. Sometimes a patient will become cold, clammy, hypotensive or even unconscious just from fear.

The patient in severe pain who is cold and clammy may be exhibiting a vaso-vagal reaction, a transient vascular and **neurogenic** reaction marked by pallor (pale appearance); nausea; cold, clammy sweating; **bradycardia** (slow heart rate) and a rapid fall in blood pressure, with eventual loss of consciousness. This is evoked by emotional stress associated with fear or severe pain.

If the patient is hot and flushed, this usually means infection but may also occur with ingestion of drugs such as **salicylates** and anticholinergics. If the patient has a bluish or blue-gray color, the patient is **cyanotic** — meaning that there is not enough oxygen in the blood, and the deoxygenated blood gives the patient a blue color. Causes of profound cyanosis include choking, **strangulation**, smothering or severe lung disease.

A yellow-orange color usually means the patient is **jaundiced**. This means that there are elevated levels of bile products in the blood, and may indicate liver or gall bladder disease, hepatitis, chemical or drug-induced liver failure, or massive breakdown of red blood cells. A cherry-red color indicates carbon monoxide poisoning but may also indicate cyanide poisoning or hypothermia. (See chapter seven on carbon monoxide poisoning.)

COLOR OF PATIENT	DIAGNOSIS
Cherry-red	Carbon monoxide poisoning (Rarely, cyanide poisoning or hypothermia)
Blue	Cyanotic (choking, asphyxiated)
Slate blue-gray	Lead poisoning
Yellow-orange	Jaundice (hepatitis, liver disease)

Smell: A smell of the patient's breath or body may help identify toxins or other medical conditions:

ODOR	TOXIN
Acetone	Ethanol, lacquer, chloroform
Acrid (pear-like)	Chloral hydrate (Noctec)
Alcohol	Ethanol, isopropyl alcohol
Almonds, bitter	Cyanide
Ammonia	Uremia (kidney failure)
Apples, rotten	Gas gangrene
Cinnamon	Pulmonary tuberculosis
Eggs, rotten	Hydrogen sulfide, mercaptans
Fish and raw liver	Liver failure, vaginitis
Foul	Bromides
Fruit	Ethanol, amyl nitrite
Garlic	Arsenic, organophosphates
Gas, stove	Carbon monoxide
Musty	Penicillin
Mothballs	Camphor
Peanuts	Vacor (rodenticide)
Putrid	Scurvy
Sewer gas	Methane
Vinegar	Acetic acid
Vinyl	Ethchlorvynol
Violets	Turpentine
Wintergreen	Methyl salicylate

CPR (Cardiopulmonary Resuscitation)

Whether the death was swift and uncontrolled (hit by a speeding car) or slow and expected (natural cause or disease), more than one-fourth of all humans will die "before their time has come" from potentially *reversible* acute processes. Their deaths could have been prevented if the proper measures had been instituted promptly.

During the 1940s, doctors in Moscow first thought of resuscitation and reviving patients with "hearts too good to die." In the United States, development of resuscitation techniques and emergency care systems began to grow and expand during the 1960s, and since then many patients with "hearts too good to die" have been salvaged.

When a patient in the hospital is found not breathing or with no pulse, a "CODE" is called. Most hospitals use a "CODE-99" or "CODE-BLUE" page to summon a crash team to the bedside. A code-team will usually include certain designated physicians (which may include cardiologists or anesthesiologists), nurses, a respiratory therapist and often a pharmacist. A crash cart containing an electrical **defibrillator** with ECG monitor, I.V. fluids, drugs and endotracheal tubes is rushed to the patient's room at the time the code is called.

The Emergency Crash Cart

The medical crash cart is a red metal cart on wheels that can be quickly moved to a patient's bedside for cardiopulmonary resuscitation. The cardiac defibrillator is kept on the top shelf and ready for use.

The cart consists of several shelves, well marked and divided according to the materials needed. The shelves are usually divided into:

1. *Medicines*: The list of drugs available on the crash cart is extensive, and includes drugs to treat cardiac arrest, shock, seizures, hemorrhage and other medical emergencies.

2. *Respiratory Therapy Supplies*: These include needed appliances for maintaining respiration, such as oral "S" airways, tubing, O_2 tubing.

3. *Surgical Supplies*: These include sutures, gauze pads, scalpels, tape, catheters, needles, syringes, tourniquets, gloves, towels.

In very rapid sequence the team will start an I.V. (intravenous line),

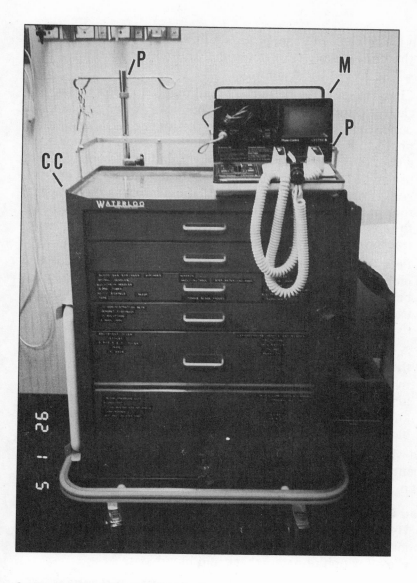

Crash cart with cardiac defibrillator.

CC — Crash cart, a red metal cart on wheels, containing everything for cardiopulmonary resuscitation
P — I.V. pole
M — Cardiac monitor for evaluating heart activity
P — Paddles for delivering DC current to the heart

attach ECG leads and charge the defibrillator, while quickly scanning the patient's chart to determine the nature of the patient's illness. The rest of the team will:

1. Check to see if the patient is breathing. If not, elevate the jaw, clear the throat of any debris. The airway of an unconscious patient is often obstructed when the tongue falls back on the pharynx. A simple way to deal with this situation is to perform a chin lift or "jaw thrust." Usually breathing resumes. If not, use an "S" airway with a bag-valve-mask and 100 percent oxygen; if the patient still is not ventilating, insert an oral-tracheal tube and manually breathe for the patient with an Ambu bag. If the airway is mechanically obstructed, then perform emergency tracheostomy to open the airway below the obstruction.

2. Feel the neck for a carotid pulse. Hook up ECG leads and monitor the electrical activity of the heart. If there is no heartbeat, begin sternal compression of the heart to pump blood; use electrical and chemical intervention to restore heart activity (defibrillator).

3. A dangerously low or absent blood pressure may indicate that there is not enough blood volume for the heart to pump effectively and maintain pressure. The intravascular volume of fluids must be increased by giving whole blood, plasma products and I.V. fluids. Drugs can be given to constrict peripheral blood vessels and further increase the pressure.

Even with all the new techniques and advances in CPR, only 2 to 10 percent of patients who "code" in the emergency room will survive. That means that 90 to 98 percent of all patients who "code" will die.

Blood Loss

Hypotension (low blood pressure) indicates a significant amount of blood loss.

Classification of hemorrhage and blood loss:

Class	Clinical Findings	% Blood Loss	Blood Volume Lost
Class I	Normal blood pressure	‹15%	‹500 cc's
Class II	Tachycardia (rapid heart rate). Normal pressure	15-30%	800-1000 cc's

Class III	"Classic Shock," low pressure, rapid heart rate (tachycardia)	30-40%	2000 cc's blood (2 Units)
Class IV	Practically Dead	›40%	

Shock

Shock is defined as a state in which a critical decrease in blood flow causes organ and tissue damage, and is usually a result of massive blood loss or very low blood pressure.

After any severe injury or blood loss, the victim may go into shock. Signs of shock include pale, bluish, clammy skin; sweating on the forehead, upper lip and palms; vomiting; and unconsciousness.

Traumatic shock is caused by loss of blood volume (massive hemorrhage). Rib, hip and pelvic fractures can puncture and tear vital organs, especially the spleen and liver, which lie beside the ribs.

If shock is not treated rapidly and reversed, there is a vicious cycle of multiple organ failure from lack of blood, a cycle that eventually causes death.

To treat shock, **paramedics** at the scene of the accident or physicians in the ER will try to raise the dangerously low blood pressure and circulating blood volume back to near normal so that the heart can pump effectively. When blood pressure is low, the victim must be kept lying down with the feet raised slightly higher than chest level (called the "Trendelenberg position"), and covered with a blanket to prevent the loss of valuable body heat. Paramedics will also be sure the airway is open and the person is breathing easily.

For a patient such as Bobby Hicks with at least a Class III hemorrhage and in shock, two units of O-negative blood would be given stat, and he would be typed and cross-matched for another six units of whole blood or packed RBC's (red blood cells). **Ringers lactate** (a solution of electrolytes and glucose) or Plasmatein (a standard sterile preparation) would be rapidly infused intravenously through large-bore needles (18-gauge or larger); drugs would then be given as needed to sustain the blood pressure.

As a General Rule

- A normal blood pressure measured on the arm with a sphygmo-manometer (blood-pressure cuff) is "120 over 80," meaning

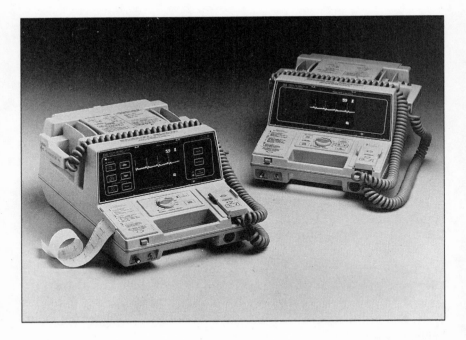

The electronic defibrillator. Hewlett-Packard Company now offers a ruggedized version of the HP 43100A and HP 43110A defibrillators to the emergency medical-services market. (PRME3000001)

120 mm Hg (millimeters of mercury) systolic (heart contraction) and 80 mm Hg diastolic (heart relaxation). It is recorded as 120/80.

- If a carotid pulse (side of the neck) is palpable, the systolic pressure is 60 mm Hg.

- A palpable femoral pulse (in the groin) correlates with pressure of 70 mm Hg.

- A palpable radial pulse (front of the wrist) correlates with a blood pressure of 80 mm Hg.

Note: When the medical staff attends to someone critical in the ER, only the systolic measurement is of immediate interest. For example, they might say, "His blood pressure is ninety."

Once these three critical factors have been corrected, attention can be turned to other injuries. The examination of the injured patient includes thorough evaluation of the head, chest and abdomen.

Types of Injury

Injuries to the head, chest or abdomen are either penetrating or nonpenetrating.

Penetrating injuries to the abdomen (stab wound, arrow, large shard of glass or bullet track) can cause sepsis and death from peritonitis and other infections if the bowel is perforated. Penetrating injuries can cause severe hemorrhage and shock if the liver, spleen, kidneys or pancreas are sliced open.

Nonpenetrating wounds result from the energy of the force applied to the body and to mechanical crushing of organs, usually resulting in a massive hemorrhage. Injuries such as a blow from a baseball bat, a fall from a ladder or a punch to the body are examples of nonpenetrating injuries.

While a nonpenetrating injury can be just as serious as a penetrating one, hemorrhage from a nonpenetrating injury can be difficult to diagnose. A girl falls from a bicycle; a young football player is tackled with a particularly hard hit; or an old man is assaulted in a dark alley with a club; all have similar complaints and symptoms, yet any one of them could be hemorrhaging from an abdominal organ laceration but have no visible external signs of injury.

Bleeding must be controlled promptly. A patient in shock with an abdominal injury (penetrating or nonpenetrating) should be operated on immediately.

Pain

When a person is brought to the emergency room with severe trauma, there is usually a "grace period" that lasts from thirty minutes to an hour during which they feel no pain. This can happen with severe injuries from auto wrecks, gunshot injuries, falls with fractures or burns, etc. Often people do not realize the extent of their injuries during this grace period, which results from a jolt to the nervous system. After the grace period, however, they may experience excruciating pain, maybe enough to send them into shock with a vaso-vagal reaction.

Examination of the Head

Head injury is a common cause of death and disability. One-third of victims admitted to hospitals for head injury are unconscious. More than 80 percent of the total deaths from head injury come from this group. More important, over 50 percent of the patients who were still able to talk at some point after their head injuries and later died, could have been saved if they had immediately received the proper treatment.

With a head injury, a physician will examine for fractures of the skull by palpating, pressing his or her fingers over areas of laceration or bruising to find cracks or depressions in the skull. The physician will look in the ears for signs of hemorrhage behind the ear drum (which would mean a fracture through the base of the skull) and examine the pupils to see if they are equal and respond appropriately to light stimulation.

If indicated, he will get an emergency CT scan (computed tomography) immediately to examine the brain and inner lining of the skull for evidence of bleeding or an expanding blood clot, a **subdural hematoma** that compresses and compromises the brain because of the confined space within the rigid skull. The subdural hematoma is from torn veins, and bleeding occurs more slowly.

Epidural bleeds are surgical emergencies, resulting from a torn artery, so the bleeding is brisk and under high pressure, causing a very rapid, life-threatening, expanding hematoma.

Pupils: "The eyes are the windows to a person's soul." A doctor can tell a lot about someone's overall general health by a careful eye examination. The retina can show changes of diabetes, arteriosclerosis, hypertension, elevated blood cholesterol and bleeding disorders, as well as certain infections.

Pupil Size

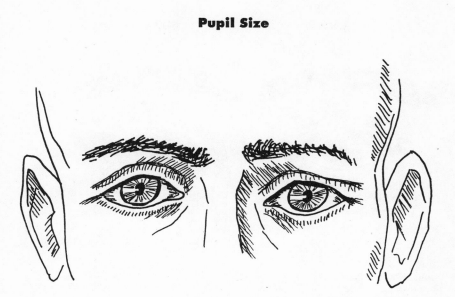

Pinpoint Pupils: Pinpoint pupils (with very sluggish, if any, response to darkness) may indicate drug usage. The drugs causing pinpoint pupils include codeine, methadone, opium, morphine, heroin and other narcotics.

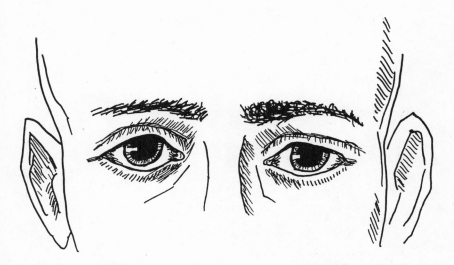

Dilated Pupils: Dilated pupils that react only sluggishly to light stimulation (that is, they do not constrict properly) are usually due to anticholinergic drugs such as an opthalmologist might use to examine eyes, including atropine and scopolamine.

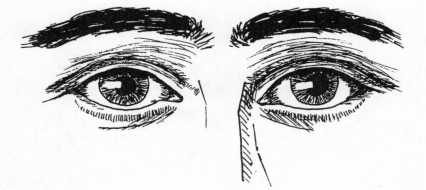

Pupils: Pupils should be the same size, and both pupils should react equally to light stimulation. In the dark, both pupils will dilate to allow more light, much as a camera lens would. In bright sunlight pupils constrict to a tiny dot.

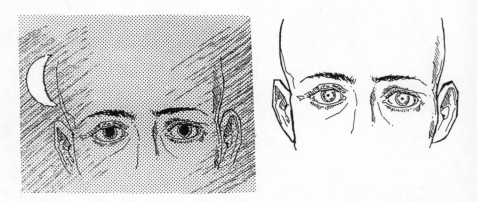

Dilated   **Constricted**

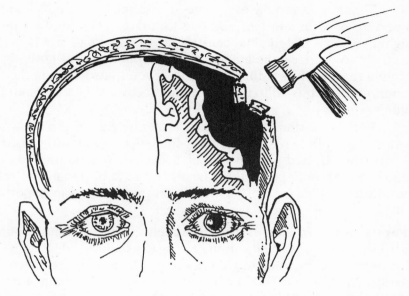

Blown Pupil: Following a severe blow to the head, there may be extensive damage to the lining of the brain and bleeding. Within the rigid confines of the skull, a growing hematoma will compress the brain. This is called a "subdural hematoma." The pupil on the side of the trauma is dilated, called a "blown pupil."

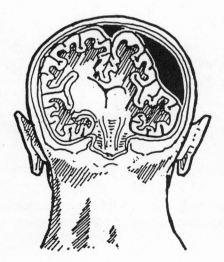

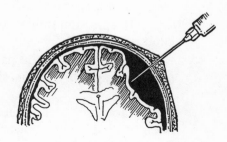

An emergency burr-hole is drilled through the skull, and the expanding hematoma is evacuated. This prevents life-threatening compression of the brain.

Pupils react rapidly to change in light intensity, much like the aperture of a camera lens, dilating to a larger size to allow more light in when it is dark, and constricting to a pinpoint size in bright sunlight to decrease the amount of light admitted. But both pupils should react equally at the same time. If you shine a light in the left pupil, both pupils will constrict simultaneously. This is a normal pupil reflex.

With head trauma, the pressure on one side of the brain will cause the pupils to react differently. Immediately following an acute injury, the affected pupil is pinpoint for a short time, then dilates and becomes much larger than the other one. A physician may refer to this as "a blown pupil." Disparity in pupil size is an important diagnostic sign.

Pupils and drug abuse: Inappropriately dilated or pinpoint pupils are usually a sign of medication or drug abuse. Large dilated pupils are seen with anticholinergic drugs, such as atropine and scopolamine. An ophthalmologist may use short-acting anticholinergics to dilate the pupils for examination.

Small, constricted pinpoint pupils are caused by narcotic use (such as codeine, methadone, opium, morphine, heroin and others). When a patient with pinpoint pupils is seen in the ER, careful attention is given to the arms and legs to look for needle tracks, burns or bruises that would indicate the patient is an I.V. drug user.

In this scene, the author incorrectly describes the changes in the pupils caused by morphine:

"Dr. Cohen to room 209. Stat"

As he rushed into room 209, he found two nurses hovering over a young woman with red hair.

"Respiration rate of six," the dark-haired nurse said. "We can't rouse her."

Cohen checked the patient's eyes. They were dilated and reacted sluggishly. "Has she received any medication?" he asked.

"Morphine!" the other nurse exclaimed. "But she hasn't been receiving any medication at all much less —"

"Vital signs," Cohen snapped. They could worry about how she got the drug later; right now they had to concentrate on saving her life.

"BP ninety over sixty, pulse sixty," the dark-haired nurse said.

"Start an IV now," he ordered. "A thousand cc's DELR, 150 cc's per hour. Put her on O$_2$, six liters per minute per nasal cannula."

"Narcan, one amp, IV now."

The drug which would counteract the morphine immediately entered Jessica Russell's bloodstream.

B.W. Battin, *Programmed for Terror* (Ballantine Books)

Pupils and brain death: The pupils provide a very rapid way to evaluate brain death: The pupils dilate to a larger-than-normal size and do not react at all to light stimulation. With anticholinergics or hallucinogenic drugs, pupils are dilated but react sluggishly to light.

When to terminate resuscitation: The decision to terminate resuscitation should be made by the physician. "Cardiac death" is evident when there has been a flat ECG line for at least thirty minutes. "Brain death" is impossible to judge during emergency resuscitation. Therefore cardiac death plus *apparent* brain death are the criteria for stopping CPR. Evaluation of the pupils is the fastest way to ascertain brain death. The decision to terminate resuscitation should be made by the physician.

As readers become more sophisticated, there is a greater demand placed on the writer to be both accurate and knowledgeable. Note how this author skillfully describes, in a few short paragraphs and with a minimum of terminology, aspects of CPR, the blue-tinged cyanotic color of a dying man, dilated pupils with absent reflexes (brain death) and a **sucking chest wound**.

Sally stared at the old man's face. He was unconscious. A blue tinge circled his lips, and beads of cold sweat glazed his forehead.

Dave Cole knelt beside her. "What have we got?" He pulled a penlight from his shirt pocket and flashed it into Hoby's eyes.

Dave ripped open the man's shirt. "Shit. We've got a sucking chest wound."

Just then Hoby gave a shuddering gasp and stopped breathing. Moving automatically, Sally pinched his nostrils shut, slid a hand under the back of his neck, lifted, and began to blow into his mouth.

Dave felt for the carotid. "Shit," he said again. He pulled Hoby's lower eyelid down and stared at the pupil. "He's dilated."

Sally caught a quick breath and breathed into Hoby's mouth.

"Let it go. He's dilated."

She raised her head and stared at him, then at the old man's eyes. His pupils were black pools that engulfed the iris. Fixed and dilated. Brain dead.

"It's no good," Dave whispered. "He's gone."

Sharon Webb, *Pestis 18* (TOR Books)

The Chest

With injury to the chest, there may be damage to the heart, the lungs, or to the great vessels that carry blood to and from the heart. Cardiac injury is usually fatal, so attention is usually given toward evaluating the lungs.

Pneumothorax and collapsed lung: If there is a tear in one of the lungs, it will collapse (**pneumothorax**). The vacuum that normally surrounds the lung fills with air and causes the lung to collapse. A **chest tube** is inserted into the thoracic cavity and the air trapped between the chest wall and lung is sucked out with continuous suction, allowing the lung to re-expand.

A large-bore chest tube (thirty-two French or larger) is inserted into the chest, between the rib and muscle chest wall and the lung, a space called the pleural space. To insert a tube, the fifth intercostal space is identified along the mid-axillary line. Straight down from the armpit (mid-axillary line) count down five rib spaces. On top of the fifth rib, a scalpel is used to make a 1" to 1½" incision, deep into the muscle that lies between the ribs. A hemostat is used to blunt-dissect the rest of the way into the chest cavity.

The chest tube is as large as the index finger, so the hole must be made large enough to accommodate it. The tube is inserted, its position checked, then connected to suction to remove air or blood that is trapped in the pleural space.

Sucking Chest Wound: If the hole in the chest wall from the injury is large enough, air is sucked in and out through it with the bellows action of breathing, and the wound is called a sucking chest wound.

A sucking chest wound can be suspected and diagnosed from the noise made by the air entering and leaving the pleural cavity of the chest. Closure of the sucking wound should be performed as soon as possible by surgical repair or application of a petroleum jelly gauze.

Flail chest: The chest cavity is a rigid structure of ribs that surrounds and protects the lungs. Fracture of more than two ribs in continuity in more than one place results in an instability of the rigid chest wall, and a "flail chest" syndrome results. The flail chest sags inward against the lungs during inspiration and compresses the lung.

If the patient will not spontaneously breathe, a tube must be inserted in the trachea and air forced into the lungs by hand using an Ambu bag or with a mechanical device called a **ventilator** (or **respirator**) that measures precisely the volume of air forced into the lungs and the rate of respiration.

In this short scene, Robin Cook has his protagonist diagnose a rupture of the heart on one of his patients at the bedside, and details how he attempts to save the man's life:

> Glancing up at the monitor, which still showed normal ECG activity, Jason touched Cedric's neck. He could feel no pulse. "Let me have a cardiac needle," he demanded. "And someone get a blood pressure." A large cardiac needle was thrust into his hand as he palpated Cedric's chest to locate the ridge of the sternum.
>
> To Jason, the diagnosis was obvious: cardiac rupture. With the ECG still being recorded, yet no pumping action of the heart, a situation of electromechanical dissociation prevailed. It could mean only one thing. The portion of Cedric's heart that had been deprived of its blood supply had split open like a squashed grape. To prove this horrendous diagnosis, Jason plunged the cardiac needle into Cedric's chest, piercing the heart's pericardial covering. When he drew back on the plunger, the syringe filled with blood.
>
> There was no doubt.
>
> Cedric's heart had burst open inside his chest.
>
> Robin Cook, *Mortal Fear* (Putnam)

The Abdomen

Injuries fall into one of two categories: penetrating or nonpenetrating.

Pneumothorax
"A Sucking Chest Wound"

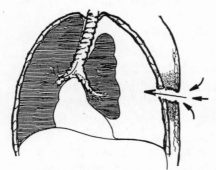 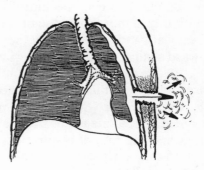

Inspiration: Air is sucked into the chest wound with inspiration.

Expiration: Air and foamy blood are sprayed out with each expiration.

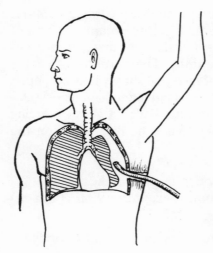

To treat a sucking chest wound with a punctured lung that is leaking air, a chest tube is placed into the pleural space between the lung and the chest wall. Then the tube is hooked to suction, and the air and blood trapped inside are removed and the lung can re-expand.

Penetrating injuries
- Stab wounds
- Gunshot wounds
- Fragmentation missiles
- Flying objects (rocks, nails hurled by lawnmower blades)
- Falls on sharp objects (picket fence)

Nonpenetrating (blunt) injuries
- Sports, industrial and injuries at home (hit or blow to the abdomen)
- Seatbelt injuries
- Blast and crush injuries

With injury to the abdomen, there is always the possibility of traumatic tear of one of the solid organs such as liver, kidney, pancreas or spleen. These are very vascular organs, and a traumatic tear can lead to massive (and often fatal) hemorrhage into the abdomen.

A very fast and simple way to test for bleeding into the abdomen is to perform a paracentesis, or peritoneal lavage. In paracentesis, a needle is inserted through the anterior (front) or lateral (side) of the abdominal wall. Sterile saline is injected, then aspirated back out (peritoneal lavage). If blood is sucked back out, there is intra-abdominal bleeding, and a **CT scan** (computerized tomography) is done to see which organ is torn. The indications for diagnostic peritoneal lavage include a history of significant blunt trauma to the abdomen or penetrating injury (stab or gunshot wound).

In most modern hospitals, a patient receives a CT scan immediately without a peritoneal lavage (paracentesis) even being performed.

A special note regarding stab wounds: If the object (arrow, spike, antenna wire, knife, pipe, stick) is still imbedded in the person, it usually is not taken out immediately upon arrival at the ER. Removing it could result in tearing of major vessels and massive bleeding that could be fatal. Only after the wound has been extensively evaluated by a surgeon is the object removed.

ER Cases Reported to Authorities
Assault

There are certain injuries seen in the ER that must be reported to the authorities. Any patient admitted to the ER with an assault injury must be reported to the police and a police report filed before the patient leaves the emergency room. Burn injuries must be reported to authorities because of the possibility of arson or intent to injure.

Injuries from hitting (fists, clubs or other objects), stabbing, shooting and burns must all be reported — even if the patient states that the injuries were accidental or self-inflicted.

Injuries That Must Be Reported

- Assault injuries
- Burns
- Accidental shooting or stabbing
- Child abuse
- DOA cases
- Rape

Child Abuse

There are over two million reported cases of child abuse per year in the United States. Most abused children are under the age of four. Generally, the younger the abused child, the greater the danger, because the incidence of death from battering is much higher in younger than older children.

Any child or infant that arrives at the ER with "suspicious" injuries (such as multiple bruises, cuts, burns or multiple fractures) must be reported and the situation carefully evaluated to determine if there is a reasonable question of child abuse. If there is evidence or strong enough suspicion of abuse, social services will intervene and remove the child from the home until the case can be investigated. The emergency physician must recognize that certain children are at immediate risk of harm and must be removed from the environment at once.

If there is a strong suspicion of abuse, the child will be admitted to the hospital, both for observation and treatment of injuries, but also to keep the child out of the home until the case can be investigated further. A child protection team will be activated, which involves the police (to investigate filing possible charges of assault) and a social caseworker who will review the home situation.

Failure to get the child out of the abusive environment could result in the death of the victim. With this realization, the parents' rights in this instance do not overshadow the child's right not to be beaten. These cases are always emotionally trying for health-care workers: They don't want to wrongfully accuse parents of child abuse, but it is better to err in favor of the child until all of the facts are known.

Here is a summary of a true case history—pathetic, disgusting and horrible—but true. I've recounted only some of the details of the case to show how important it is that all cases of suspected child abuse be reported:

> A grocery store clerk watched as the three-year-old boy was struck severely in the face, then heard his mother tell him he would get the beating of his life when he got home. When he got home, the child was beaten, and the boyfriend grabbed him by the hair, ripping hair from his scalp. Two weeks later, the little boy was dead, and his mother and her boyfriend charged with murder.

> Since the age of two, the child was often seen bruised and with large chunks of hair missing from his head. The previous winter the child had frostbitten hands, with the skin peeling from them. That spring, the child was taken from the home, and the mother and boyfriend charged with "child endangerment." But that charge was dropped and the child returned to the home, only to die a few months later.

> After one severe beating, the little boy kept throwing up, falling down, and holding his stomach. The mother did not seek medical attention for him, and he died of peritonitis from a ruptured intestine; an autopsy also revealed a skull fracture, massive swelling of the face and multiple bruises.

Rape

A rape case presented to the emergency room is usually treated by strict guidelines established to help the victim and to gather information for prosecution and conviction.

Here is the usual protocol that is followed:

First, the police are contacted. An officer (or detective) will come to the emergency room and bring a sealed rape kit that remains the property of the police. The victim will be questioned, then examined by a physician and nurse. The seal to the kit is broken; inside are a series of envelopes and sealed cotton swabs.

Envelope 1: Contains a paper towel and a comb. The towel is placed under the buttocks of the victim; the comb is used to comb the pubic hairs for evidence. Then the towel with the combings along with the comb is returned to the envelope; it is sealed, initialed and dated.

Envelope 2: Any other debris (glass, dirt or blood) is scraped from the patient's clothes or body and put into the envelope. It is sealed, initialed and dated.

Envelope 3: A thin file is used to scrape all material from under the fingernails, then the fingernails are cut, and the clippings and scrapings are put into the envelope, sealed, initialed and dated.

Envelope 4: Twelve hairs from the scalp are cut for evidence. The twelve hairs are put into the envelope, sealed, initialed and dated.

Envelope 5: Twelve pubic hairs of the victim are then cut, put into the envelope and sealed.

Envelope 6: The victim's sputum is collected onto a filter; put into the envelope and sealed.

Envelope 7: Cotton swabs are used to wipe around the external portion of the genitalia and the vulva, then put into the envelope, which is then sealed.

Envelope 8: Internal swabs are obtained from the oral, anal and vaginal mucosa, then the swabs are sealed in the envelope.

Envelope 9: A blood sample of the victim is obtained, 10 cc's of blood are drawn into a red-stoppered tube, which is labeled, initialed, dated and sealed.

Next, another swab is taken from the vagina, and a smear is made onto a glass slide and immediately examined for mobile sperm.

Finally, the victim is examined very carefully, looking for injuries such as bruising or tearing of the vagina, bites or teeth marks anywhere on the body; a description of the findings is noted.

Everything is again placed inside the box, sealed, initialed and dated, then turned over to the police right then and there. The sealed kit becomes legal property in police custody. This very rigid policy is followed so that there is no breakdown in the chain of command of evidence and to ensure that the prosecution of the case is in no way jeopardized.

Summary of Rape Kit and Hospital Procedure

- Police bring a sealed box to the hospital.
- At the hospital, the seal is broken in the presence of the police.
- The kit contains swabs, envelopes, tubes for blood, a comb and forms for describing injuries.
- Everything is initialed, returned to the box, the box is sealed again, signed and dated by the physician, and handed back to the police; it is now official legal police property.

DOA (Dead on Arrival)

A patient who is brought to the hospital dead on arrival (**DOA**) is another reportable event for the emergency physician. All DOA cases must be reported to the **medical examiner** (or **coroner's** office) for investigation of possible foul play and to determine whether an **autopsy** is indicated. Only those cases determined to warrant further investigation will then be autopsied or studied (blood samples, drug levels, toxicology tests, etc).

It is the emergency physician's responsibility in the case of the DOA to pronounce the patient dead. Nothing should be done by the emergency department staff to alter the appearance of the corpse since this only complicates the subsequent medical-legal investigation.

If a person arrives DOA or dies after arrival to the emergency room from injuries due to gunshot, stabbing or other assault, it becomes an immediate coroner's case. First the coroner is contacted, then the police.

The body is not altered or disturbed further, because this could destroy valuable evidence. In the case of gunshot death, paper bags are slipped over the hands of the victims to protect trace evidence, such as gunpowder residue, if present. (Do *not* use plastic bags to cover the hands, because the moisture from the skin will ruin powder residue).

The coroner and an officer or detective will arrive to investigate. Usually, the body is photographed from every possible angle before it is further disturbed, then taken to the coroner's **morgue** for autopsy at a later time.

The physician in the emergency room will declare a person dead by noting the time and recording it on a chart, but will *not* sign a **death certificate**. This is almost always done by the coroner's office (on rare occasions, the death certificate may be signed by the victim's personal attending physician). See chapter three for further discussion of this.

Death in the ER

All deaths in the ER will be reported to the coroner's office. In the case of Bobby Hicks, the coroner and photographer would have gone to the Emergency Room immediately after his death was reported to the coroner's office. After photographing his body from every possible angle, his hands would be covered with paper bags and his body transported by ambulance to the coroner's morgue for a complete medical-legal autopsy.

Summary of the Bobby Hicks Case

- Arrived in the emergency room with a sucking chest wound from a gunshot wound to the chest; hemorrhage; and shock.
- Had a cardiac arrest, and ER staff performed CPR for forty minutes, but efforts were unsuccessful and he died.
- He was pronounced dead by Dr. Parks, the attending ER physician, at exactly 2:31 A.M., forty minutes *after* he coded with cardiac arrest.
- The coroner's office and the police department were both notified, and the body carefully placed to the side without further disturbing it.
- A police detective and the coroner arrived and began their investigation of a homicide.

- The coroner had the body photographed from every possible angle, then the body was wrapped to preserve evidence.
- The body was identified by family (either in the ER at the hospital, or later at the morgue).
- The body was transported by ambulance to the morgue to await a complete medical-legal autopsy. Once at the morgue, the body was weighed, measured, photographed dressed and nude, X-rayed and prepared for an autopsy.

Where to Go for More Information

Call a hospital near you to talk with both a nurse and a physician. ERs go from a dead zone with nothing happening to complete chaos with critically ill patients arriving in clusters. It is impossible to tell when the ER will be quiet, but Sunday morning is a good bet. Ask if you might visit during this time to talk with one of the nurses or physicians. If they are not busy, they will probably accommodate you. You might also ask to sit in the ER during a busy Friday night to observe and take notes.

You can also visit a local fire station to talk with the paramedics. They may let you review the emergency equipment and describe its use to you. You might ask them to recount any interesting emergency cases they recall that might be of interest to you.

Numerous first-aid emergency treatment books that can answer basic questions for you are available in most bookstores. You might also consider taking or observing a CPR course offered in your community.

You could watch a few episodes (or reruns) of popular medical television shows such as "Rescue 911" or "St. Elsewhere." You may get new ideas or see a particular emergency procedure played out.

DECLARED DEAD

The law requires a physician or the coroner or medical examiner to certify the **cause of death**. But there is no law requiring that the actual pronouncement of death must be made by a physician. It is common practice in hospitals and nursing homes for a competent nurse to pronounce death and notify the physician. Also, an ambulance team or police official may determine death of an individual.

There are exceptions to this.

When a person arrives at the hospital emergency room DOA (dead on arrival), a physician must declare the person dead. The DOA will automatically become a coroner's case and will be transported to a coroner's morgue for consideration of an autopsy.

When a condemned person is executed within the prison system, an attending physician must declare that person dead. This assures that the execution has been successful and that the legal intent of the death sentence has been properly performed.

The Legal Time of Death

When a person is declared dead, the exact time must be recorded for legal purposes. The term "time of death" refers to the **legal time of death**, and is the moment that a professional person first sees the body and declares it to be dead. That time is recorded on the death certificate. (See chapter five on "estimated" time of death.)

For example, if a body is discovered in an alley, and it is obvious that the person has been dead for several weeks, the legal time of death is still the exact time that the police or coroner arrive on the scene and pronounce that person dead. The legal time of death that is recorded does *not* take into account how long the person has been dead, only the moment the body is discovered and the time recorded.

If a person comes to the ER with clinical death and the ER staff begins CPR resuscitation, the *legal time of death* is the moment the physician in charge stops CPR and the person is pronounced dead.

Bobby Hicks came to the ER unconscious and in shock, then had a cardiac arrest. A code was called and CPR was performed for forty minutes. The time of death for Bobby Hicks was the moment that CPR was stopped and he was declared dead, forty minutes after the cardiac arrest.

Who Has the Authority to Pronounce a Person Dead?

Hospice and Home Death

The family physician, a registered nurse or a paramedic may declare the person dead, then record the legal time of death after their arrival on the scene. The body will usually be transported directly to a **funeral home** without any further medical-legal intervention.

Nursing Home Death

A physician or registered nurse may declare the person dead, then record the legal time of death. A family physician who has attended to the deceased may declare the cause of death to be natural causes secondary to old age. Or, if circumstances are complicated or not as clear-cut, a coroner may be asked to rule on the cause of death, either with or without an autopsy.

Attended Death in the Hospital

A physician in attendance must declare the person dead in the hospital, then record the legal time of death. If the death occurred during medical treatment or a surgical procedure, then it becomes a coroner's case to determine cause of death.

Discovered Body or Unattended Death

A professional person (police officer, paramedic, nurse or physician) arriving on the scene may declare the person dead, and then record the legal time of death. However, a coroner is almost always required to make a ruling as to the cause of death.

Death Occurring During Transport in Ambulance

Medical treatment will usually continue until the patient arrives at a medical facility. Medical staff will then determine that further resuscitative efforts be discontinued and the person declared dead.

The Death Certificate

The death certificate is an official document stating the cause of death and the legal time of death. It must be signed by a physician or coroner and then filed in the county where death occurred (or where the body was found). All death certificates are a part of the official county records and can be reviewed upon request.

The death certificate must be filed before final disposition of the body. Neither burial nor cremation can proceed until this has been done. If the cause of death was questionable, or the results of tests are not yet in, the physician would then write under Cause of Death, "Pending." If the cause of death is later established, it is then filled in. But, either the cause of death or "pending" must be put on the death certificate to complete it.

When the **manner of death** is not due to natural causes, a simple statement is required on the death certificate to indicate how the fatal incident occurred: "Deceased shot self," "Deceased hit tree while driving automobile," "Deceased shot by other person."

If an **attended death** occurs in the hospital, the physician fills out the death certificate, then the hospital files it with the county. If an unattended death occurs, either a physician or a coroner will rule on the cause of death, and then fill out and file the death certificate. Any death that is questionable, sudden, unusual or violent, including accidental death and suicide, must have the death certificate completed by the coroner after the results of the autopsy are known. (Or, if autopsy results are incomplete, "pending" is inserted until all information is known).

While a paramedic or nursing home official may pronounce someone dead, a death certificate must be completed by either a physician or a coroner.

Fetal Death (Miscarriage)

A miscarriage in which the fetus weighs 500 grams or less (less than 1.1 pounds), even if it is alive for a brief period of time after delivery, does *not* require a death certificate. The fetus is nonviable and is considered a surgical specimen.

However, a special fetal death certificate is required by almost all states when the fetus weighs more than 500 grams. Fetal death must be registered (by means of the death certificate) when the fetus weighs more than 500 grams and is born dead.

If the fetus weighs more than 500 grams and is born alive, even if only momentarily, then a regular death certificate is filed. However, an autopsy is not mandated by law. (See also pages 89-90 for further discussion of this.)

If a miscarriage occurs unattended and outside the hospital, a physician should be called, since unattended fetal death could require a coroner's investigation.

Completing the Death Certificate

There are only a few circumstances where a physician other than the coroner may fill out and complete the death certificate, and they include the following:

- A person dies of a known terminal disease while under the care of the physician.

- An elderly person dies in a nursing home where they have been under the care and supervision of a physician.

- An attended death in the hospital, not during treatment or surgical procedure.

- A death at home, through the **hospice** program, where the physician knows the patient and of the terminal disease.

- A sudden death in an individual who has been undergoing

Ohio Department of Health

VITAL STATISTICS
CERTIFICATE OF DEATH

DO NOT WRITE IN MARGIN RESERVED FOR ODH DATA CODING

Reg. Dist. No. _____
Primary Reg. Dist. No. _____

State File No. _____
Registrar's No. _____

a. _____
b. _____
c. _____
d. _____
e. _____

DECEDENT

1. DECEDENT'S NAME (First, Middle, LAST)		2. SEX	3. DATE OF DEATH (Month, Day, Year)

4. SOCIAL SECURITY NUMBER	5a. AGE - Last Birthday (Years)	5b. UNDER 1 YEAR		5c. UNDER 1 DAY		6. DATE OF BIRTH (Month, Day, Year)	7. BIRTHPLACE (City and State or Foreign Country)
		Months	Days	Hours	Minutes		

8. WAS DECEDENT EVER IN U.S. ARMED FORCES? ☐ Yes ☐ No	9a. PLACE OF DEATH (Check only one)

HOSPITAL: ☐ Inpatient ☐ ER/Outpatient ☐ DOA   OTHER: ☐ Nursing Home ☐ Residence ☐ Other (Specify)

9b. FACILITY NAME (If not institution, give street and number)	9c. CITY, VILLAGE, TWP., OR LOCATION OF DEATH	9d. COUNTY OF DEATH

IF DEATH OCCURRED IN INSTITUTION, GIVE RESIDENCE BEFORE ADMISSION

10. MARITAL STATUS - Married, Never Married, Widowed, Divorced (Specify)	11. SURVIVING SPOUSE (If wife, give maiden name)	12a. DECEDENT'S USUAL OCCUPATION (Give kind of work done during most of working life. Do not use retired.)	12b. KIND OF BUSINESS/INDUSTRY

13a. RESIDENCE - STATE	13b. COUNTY	13c. CITY, TOWN, TWP., OR LOCATION	13d. STREET AND NUMBER

13e. INSIDE CITY LIMITS? (Yes or No)	13f. ZIP CODE	14. WAS DECEDENT OF HISPANIC ORIGIN? (Specify No or Yes - If yes, specify Cuban, Mexican, Puerto Rican, etc.) ☐ No ☐ Yes Specify:	15. RACE - American Indian, Black, White, etc. (Specify)	16. DECEDENT'S EDUCATION (Specify only highest grade completed)
				Elementary/Secondary (0-12)	College (1-4 or 5+)

PARENTS

17. FATHER'S NAME (First, Middle, Last)	18. MOTHER'S NAME (First, Middle, Maiden Surname)

INFORMANT

19a. INFORMANT'S NAME (Type/Print)	19b. MAILING ADDRESS (Street and Number or Rural Route Number, City or Town, State, Zip Code)

DISPOSITION

20a. METHOD OF DISPOSITION ☐ Burial ☐ Cremation ☐ Removal from State ☐ Donation ☐ Other (Specify)	20b. PLACE OF DISPOSITION (Name of cemetery, crematory, or other place)	20c. LOCATION - City or Town, State

20d. DATE OF DISPOSITION	21a. NAME OF EMBALMER	21b. LICENSE NUMBER

22a. SIGNATURE OF FUNERAL DIRECTOR OR OTHER PERSON ►	22b. LICENSE NUMBER (of Licensee)	23. NAME AND ADDRESS OF FACILITY

REGISTRAR

24. REGISTRAR'S SIGNATURE ►	25. DATE FILED (Month, Day, Year)

26a. SIGNATURE OF PERSON ISSUING PERMIT ►	26b. DIST. No.	27. DATE PERMIT ISSUED

f. _____
g. _____
h. _____
i. _____

CERTIFIER

28a. CERTIFIER (Check only one)	☐ CERTIFYING PHYSICIAN To the best of my knowledge, death occurred at the time, date and place, and due to the cause(s) and manner as stated

☐ CORONER On the basis of examination and/or investigation, in my opinion, death occurred at the time, date, and place, and due to the cause(s) and manner as stated.

28b. TIME OF DEATH M	28c. DATE PRONOUNCED DEAD (Month, Day, Year)	28d. WAS CASE REFERRED TO CORONER? ☐ Yes ☐ No

j. _____
k. _____
l. _____
m. _____

28e. SIGNATURE AND TITLE OF CERTIFIER ►	28f. LICENSE NUMBER	28g. DATE SIGNED (Month, Day, Year)

29. NAME AND ADDRESS OF PERSON WHO COMPLETED CAUSE OF DEATH (Type/Print)

n. _____
o. _____
p. _____
q. _____
r. _____
s. _____
t. _____
u. _____

CAUSE OF DEATH

SEE INSTRUCTIONS ON OTHER SIDE

30. PART I. Enter the diseases, injuries, or complications that caused the death. Do not enter the mode of dying, such as cardiac or respiratory arrest, shock, or heart failure. List only one cause on each line. TYPE OR PRINT IN PERMANENT INK

Approximate Interval Between Onset and Death

IMMEDIATE CAUSE (Final disease or condition resulting in death) → a. _____ DUE TO (OR AS A CONSEQUENCE OF):

Sequentially list conditions, if any, leading to immediate cause. Enter UNDERLYING CAUSE (Disease or injury that initiated events resulting in death) LAST

b. _____ DUE TO (OR AS A CONSEQUENCE OF):

c. _____ DUE TO (OR AS A CONSEQUENCE OF):

d. _____

PART II. Other significant conditions contributing to death but not resulting in the underlying cause given in Part I.	31a. WAS AN AUTOPSY PERFORMED?	31b. WERE AUTOPSY FINDINGS AVAILABLE PRIOR TO COMPLETION OF CAUSE OF DEATH?
	Yes No	Yes No

32 MANNER OF DEATH ☐ Natural ☐ Pending Investigation ☐ Accident ☐ Suicide ☐ Could not be Determined ☐ Homicide	33a. DATE OF INJURY (Month, Day, Year)	33b. TIME OF INJURY M	33c. INJURY AT WORK? ☐ Yes ☐ No	33d. DESCRIBE HOW INJURY OCCURRED
	33e. PLACE OF INJURY - At home, farm, street, factory, office building, etc. (Specify)			33f. LOCATION (Street and Number or Rural Route Number, City or Town, State)

TYPE OR PRINT IN PERMANENT INK

HEA 2717 5152.06 Rev. 2/89

Sample death certificate.

medical treatment by a physician. For instance, if a person has known severe coronary artery disease, and is being seen regularly by a physician to treat it, then suddenly collapses and dies, the primary physician may sometimes be permitted to complete the death certificate.

Almost all other cases require a ruling by the coroner to determine the legal cause of death.

F O U R
How the Body Is Handled

Here is a chronological account of procedures followed after the discovery of a dead body or immediately after someone dies.

Sequence of Events After Death

1. A body is discovered.
2. The body is pronounced dead by the appropriate person, usually a physician, but sometimes by a nurse or a paramedic.
3. The body is sent to the morgue or funeral home, identified by family or friends, and tagged.
4. Either the attending physician determines the cause of death, or the coroner evaluates the death and determines if an autopsy is required to establish the cause of death.
5. If indicated, a medical-legal autopsy is performed.
6. The death certificate is filled out, stating the cause of death after determined by the autopsy.

7. All of the materials obtained (autopsy report, photographs, toxicology test results and opinion) are turned over to the authorities and become a part of the **Corpus Delicti,** or "body of evidence."

8. The body is then turned over to the family and becomes the property and responsibility of the next of kin for either **cremation** or **embalming** and burial.

Various Possibilities Following a Death

Unattended Death in a Nursing Home or Death Following Chronic Illness

Sample cases

- An elderly person dies unattended in a nursing home.
- A person with a known fatal illness dies in a hospital.
- A young mother with a long-standing chronic illness dies unattended at home before the hospice nurse arrives.
- An eighty-three-year-old man apparently dies in his sleep in bed and is discovered two days later.

The procedure following these deaths would be:

1. The body is pronounced dead by a physician or registered nurse.

2. The cause of death is presumed by circumstances and requires no further investigation.

3. A death certificate is signed.

4. The body is sent to a funeral home.

5. The body is turned over to the family for burial or cremation. If the family elects cremation, they must wait at least forty-eight hours after the person died in case there may be any investigation into the cause of death.

Sudden, Unexpected Death Following Trauma

Sample cases

- A farmer's tractor rolls over on him and he is crushed to death.
- Four teenagers are killed in an automobile crash.

The procedure following these deaths would be:

1. The body is pronounced dead by a physician, police officer or paramedic at the scene.
2. The coroner's office is contacted and an investigator is sent to the scene.
3. The body is taken to a funeral home or morgue.
4. Blood is drawn to test for alcohol and drugs for initial assessment.
5. A medical-legal autopsy is usually required.
6. A ruling is made and a death certificate completed and signed.
7. The body is released to the family for burial or cremation.

A Sudden, Unexpected Nontraumatic Death

Sample cases

- A healthy man of fifty falls over dead of a presumed sudden heart attack.
- A teenage girl is found drowned in a bathtub.
- An elderly woman is killed from a fall down the cellar steps.
- A farmer is found dead in the barn from a gunshot wound to the head, possibly self-inflicted.
- A forty-two-year-old man dies on the operating table while undergoing coronary bypass surgery.
- A man is seriously injured in a boating accident; although attended to by paramedics, he is dead on arrival at the ER (DOA).
- A person is found dead lying beside the highway.
- A known alcoholic who lives in back alleys is found dead late one night.
- A sixteen-year-old boy is shot to death during the robbery of an all-night convenience store.

The procedure following these deaths would be:

1. The body is pronounced dead by a physician or police officer at the scene.
2. The coroner's office is contacted and an investigator sent to the scene.
3. The body is taken to a morgue designated by the coroner.

4. A complete medical-legal autopsy is performed.

5. A ruling is made and a death certificate is completed and signed.

6. An opinion is given and all the evidence is turned over to the court. This material constitutes the corpus delicti.

7. The body is only then released to the family for burial or cremation.

Although every type of death is not covered, you should now be able to place any death used in your plot into one of the three categories and then appropriately "handle the body" in the subsequent scenes.

Disposal of the Body

Historical and Religious Background

After the body has been declared dead and a death certificate signed, the body is turned over to the family for burial or cremation. Varying attitudes around the world toward death and dying are reflected in the many ways that the dead are disposed. Most burial customs reflect two factors: a belief in life after death, and a belief that death brings a close contact with evil spirits.

Since primitive times, people have been afraid of the dead. Deep-seated fears, superstitions and religious beliefs govern how the dead are handled. Magic, prayers, sacrifices and varied religious customs developed because of the belief that death and the dead body were somehow linked with evil demons and angry gods; that even in death the deceased would have to do battle with evil spirits and demons. Even today, burial customs reflect this belief. All cultures have devised ways of dealing with their dead and the perceived evil spirits associated with them.

Ancient Aztecs believed that life is a dream from which Death awakens us. They respected death as an integral part of life. On All Saints Day and All Souls Day, Mexicans still celebrate and honor the dead with flowers and food for the graves; some don Devil's clothing or wear skull masks; some hang skeleton mobiles in storefronts. The celebration mixes respect for and fear of death, and always ends with dancing in the streets, laughing, drinking, singing — as if the celebration of death could eliminate it.

Many burial customs throughout the centuries indicate a concern with life after death. The dead have been buried with possessions, weapons and food, all pointing to a belief in an afterlife.

Everyone alive must face the same inevitable fact "from dust we came, to dust we shall return." But how different cultures choose to get the dead back to dust varies greatly. Each has developed a unique set of laws or customs relating to the handling of the dead and the preparation of the body for the grave.

Archeology suggests that cremation was first used during the Stone Age. In Tibet, bodies are sunk in water. The Sioux Indians of North America put their dead on high platforms. And a religious group in India, the Parsis, took their dead to enclosures and let birds pick the body clean.

Cremation

The use of fire to dispose of the dead is not new. Prehistoric people used fire, a miracle from the gods, to cremate bodies as far back as the Stone Age. The Greeks began using it around 1000 B.C., and the Bible reports the cremation of Saul in the book of Samuel: "and took the body of Saul and the bodies of his sons from the wall of Beth-Shan, and burnt them there."

The Vikings, Romans, people of ancient India and Buddhists all used cremation for the dead. Cremation is the almost exclusive method used by Hindus of India. Traditional Orthodox Jewish culture forbids cremation, but the Catholic Church recently removed its ban and many Catholics now choose church-sanctioned cremation.

Cremation in the United States has grown steadily. In 1884 there were forty-one cremations in the U.S., but now there are several hundred thousand cremations annually. Great Britain and Japan lead the world in the number of cremations annually. In Great Britain, less than a third of all corpses are buried.

Requirements: Most crematories require a rigid, combustible container for the body (usually wood). It is important to remove pacemakers (an electrical device to trigger and regulate the heart rate) from the body before cremation, since the lithium batteries can explode and pollute the environment.

Many states require a person be deceased for forty-eight hours prior to cremation. This is to ensure that any investigation of the cause of death can be instigated if needed. Obviously, once the body is cremated, it cannot be studied further.

Once the casket is rolled into the cremation chamber, incineration occurs at temperatures of 1800° Fahrenheit or higher. Crematories most commonly use natural gas to produce the intense heat, but oil, propane gas or electricity can also be used as fuel. The combustion chamber, big enough to hold only one coffin at a time, is lined with fire bricks that can withstand heat up to 3500° Fahrenheit.

Cremation is usually performed at 1800°; total time for cremation takes sixty to ninety minutes, depending on the weight of the body. When the cremation is complete, the white-hot brick furnace must cool down before the remains of ash and pieces of bone (weighing three to seven pounds, depending on body weight) are removed. Bone fragments are then collected and pulverized in a grinding machine to the size of granulated sugar.

The **cremains** are then collected in an urn and delivered to the funeral home. The ashes may be mailed but must be shipped registered mail. More than eight thousand Americans die abroad each year, and cremation (with the remains mailed back to the U.S.) is a convenient way of handling the body. There are no restrictions regarding the handling or resting place of cremains.

Similar to the celebrations and dancing on All Souls Day, some people in America have found new ways to honor the dead. In California, funerals have become more of a celebration of living than a mournful cry for the dead. Some choose to drop the cremated remains over the side of boats into the bay, followed by a handful of flowers that bob on the waves. Everything has been tried, from picnics to wine-tasting parties to garden parties with hors d'oeuvres and valet parking.

In the mountains of Idaho, some choose to load ashes into cartridges and fire the remains into the sky to be scattered by the winds.

Embalming

Egyptians began embalming the bodies of the wealthy as early as 4000 B.C. The bodies were soaked in carbonate of soda, and the intestines and brain removed, and salt and herbs packed into the body cavities.

In early nineteenth-century America, embalming also served to assure that no one was buried accidently "while in a trance." There was no doubt that the body was dead after embalming. The Civil War brought embalming to most funeral homes in this country, a custom that remains even today. It prevented decomposition and smell until the bodies could be sent back to their families for burial. Sanitation to halt the spread of disease was also a consideration at the time.

Today embalming serves to postpone decomposition and allows the body to be transported and viewed by the family before burial. It preserves the body, eradicates the smell of decomposing flesh, and helps restore a somewhat lifelike appearance. However, since the Civil War, embalming remains almost exclusively an American tradition — it is rarely used in Europe.

Methods: Embalming methods have not changed in the past one hundred years. On a table, the limbs are massaged to counter **rigor mortis**, then an artery and vein beside each other (in the armpit, neck or groin) are cut open. The process consists of draining the blood, then filling veins with a preservative — a formaldehyde-based, blood-colored fluid. A large-bore needle is inserted in the naval (umbilicus) through which blood and waste are pumped from the abdominal cavity. Then it is filled with about eight to ten pints of preserving fluid.

Embalming takes about an hour and a half, and the effects are dramatic. The deathly pallor and greenish discoloration disappear, and there is no longer the odor of death.

Funeral directors make every effort to improve the rapidly declining appearance, to give the impression of peaceful sleep instead of death and decay.

After bathing and embalming the body, the beard will be shaved (on males). The eyes that have sunk back because of loss of vitreous fluid will have small pads placed under the eyelids to restore a lifelike bulge. The mouth is stuffed with cotton and stitched shut. The lips are smoothed to give the impression of relaxation with a faint smile. Makeup is applied, and finally, the body is dressed.

The fingers of the hands are gently tugged until they assume a pose suggesting peace and rest. It is the dead person's hands that most people are likely to touch during a wake or funeral service.

Burial

Burial is the most common method of disposal of the dead for Christians, Jews and Muslims. Burial developed from the belief that the dead will rise again. Like a seed, the body is planted in the earth to await rebirth.

Regulations: Unlike cremation, which has no laws regarding the handling and disposal of cremains, there are rigid laws concerning burial. These laws reflect both religious customs as well as health considerations and the prevention of spread of contagious diseases. Cemeteries require that a grave liner (concrete slabs) or coffin vaults be used. In the United States, the inside of the coffin is lined with copper or zinc, and the lid is screwed shut before burial.

Home burial is possible in some rural areas, depending on local laws. Burial must be some distance from a water supply, and grave-yards become *permanent* easement on the property and may de-crease the value of the land at sale. That prevents a family from burying grandpa in the backyard of the farm, then selling the prop-erty and allowing someone to farm over the grave. The home grave-site must remain a grave-site. In those circumstances when construc-tion must proceed over a grave-site, the body must be removed and placed in another appropriate grave.

There are no laws concerning embalming prior to burial, and it is now performed almost by custom in the United States. But embalming still remains an option that family members may elect not to use prior to burial.

Funeral Director (Mortician)

Being a mortician is one of the oldest professions in the world. But who becomes a mortician? Interesting enough, more than 95 percent of those who choose to become morticians had significant personal contact with funeral directors prior to considering it as a way of life. The contact could be anything from mowing their lawn to knowing them in church. But recruiting for the mortician industry is definitely a grass-roots phenomenon.

That is because most people have heard myths about funeral directors and mortuaries, and focus only on the aspect of dealing with dead bodies. Other duties include comforting the bereaved's family and marketing caskets. While starting salaries average about $25,000 a year, six-figure incomes are possible after building up the business.

Requirements: Almost all states require funeral directors and em-balmers to complete a course in mortuary science, which ranges from nine months to three years, followed by an apprenticeship of one to three years. This varies greatly from state to state: Ohio demands four years of college, but in California you don't need any formal education to become a funeral director. Colorado has virtually no funeral home regulations but does require a certification of competency in mortuary science.

The American Board of Funeral Service Education accredits and oversees more than forty mortuary schools nationwide. The students learn how to embalm, how to restore damaged faces using wax and makeup with details obtained from photographs, how to market caskets and how to comfort the bereaved family.

The Coroner and Medical Examiner

There are two types of medical-legal investigative systems currently in the United States: the coroner and the medical examiner (ME). Approximately twelve states currently have a coroner system, twenty-two have medical examiners, and sixteen have both a coroner and medical examiner. The trend is for the coroner system to be replaced by the medical examiner.

There is confusion between the terms *coroner* and *medical examiner*. While under certain states' laws they may be synonymous, they are in fact separate titles. In some states the medical examiner is also the coroner, but in other states the medical examiner is appointed by the coroner to conduct the medical autopsy and to offer an official **opinion** for evidence.

The Coroner

The coroner is an elected public official whose duty is to oversee the mechanics of obtaining a medical-legal investigation of death. In some states, anyone may run for the office and be elected coroner — even without any formal education in forensic medicine. In some areas of the country, in fact, the coroner can be a funeral director.

A coroner with no formal education in forensic medicine will appoint a **forensic pathologist** who then functions as medical examiner. Or, if the state has both a coroner and medical examiner, the ME will examine a case and give the findings to the elected coroner, who will then render a coroner's report.

An elected coroner may appoint a deputy coroner to assist in the medical-legal investigation and to perform autopsies. The deputy coroner is almost always a qualified forensic pathologist, the same as a medical examiner.

Medical Examiner

A medical examiner is a physician who has specialized in a specific branch of pathology called forensic medicine and is trained in the legal investigation of death. The medical examiner is appointed either by the court or a coroner. The ME has the authority of the appropriate court officials to perform a medical-legal autopsy and render an opinion as to the cause, manner and mode of death.

Most states have now changed the law so that anyone running for the office of coroner must also be a forensic pathologist (and in this instance, the coroner and medical examiner will be the same individual).

This change is happening across the country and now almost all coroners are trained forensic pathologists, and the terms coroner and medical examiner are the same in qualification and training.

CORONER: A county or city official elected by popular vote. May or may not be a qualified forensic pathologist, depending on local laws.

DEPUTY CORONER: An appointed position, usually selected by the coroner.

MEDICAL EXAMINER: An appointed position, usually by the court.

Note: While the deputy coroner and medical examiner are qualified forensic pathologists, the coroner may or may not be, depending on local laws.

TIME OF DEATH

Determination of Time of Death

The *estimated time of death* is the time when death actually occurred. The *legal time of death* (the time that is recorded on the death certificate) is the time at which the body was discovered. Therefore, the estimated time of death may be days or weeks earlier than the legal time of death.

Knowing the estimated time when death occurred is one of the most important factors in a murder case. It may convict a murderer, break an alibi or eliminate a suspect. But determination of the time of death is difficult because so many factors affect the rate at which postmortem changes develop. In fact, it is impossible to establish an *exact* time of death. Only a reasonable estimation can be made, usually within a range of hours or days at best.

Generally speaking, the sooner after death a body is found, the more accurate this estimation can be. However, it is still impossible to fix the exact hour and minute of death unless it was witnessed.

Three sources are commonly used to determine the time of death:

1. *Witnesses*
2. *Postmortem changes of the body*
   a. temperature of the body
   b. the degree of rigidity (rigor mortis)
   c. the degree of discoloration of the skin (**livor mortis**)
   d. the degree of decomposition of the body
   e. chemical changes in the eye
3. *Associated events*
   a. scene "markers" (newspapers, TV schedules, letters)

Postmortem Changes

Just as dying is a process that leads to death, the body's decomposition following death is a process. Estimating the time of death depends on changes that occur at different times during the decomposition process.

To maintain itself during life, the human body supplies oxygen to all the tissues, provides for removal of waste, and defends itself from bacteria that are present in the body. However, at the moment of death, all these systems stop. Bacteria begin to grow, releasing enzymes that dissolve the body from the inside and produce gas. Blood turns a dark purplish color from loss of oxygen and, under the pull of gravity, settles to the dependent portions (the underside) of the body. Muscles begin to stiffen. These are the **postmortem** decomposition changes.

When a body is discovered, it must be examined immediately on the spot and the findings recorded. Hours later, after it has been photographed, put into a body bag, transported to a morgue and put into a cooler, the postmortem changes will be different and more advanced. The sooner after death a body is examined, the more accurate is the estimation of time of death.

All of the body's postmortem changes are affected by environmental factors, which must be included in the determination of the time of death. Decomposition is greatly accelerated in hot, tropical temperatures, and is slowed in cold temperatures. Bodies of early explorers have been found under the polar ice, preserved as if they had died yesterday. Conversely, in the jungle, burial is performed almost the moment a person dies because the decomposition and rotting of the body, as well as invasion of insects, begins immediately and progresses rapidly. In a moist, tropical climate, a corpse can become skeletonized in a few short weeks.

Insect Detectives

According to a report in *U.S. News & World Report*, insects provide a precise method for determining the time of death. Forensic entomology is the study of insects associated with death. These forensic entomologists think that the death of a human triggers a very predictable insect activity that can be traced backward in time. When death occurs, there is a universal death scent, which attracts hundreds of insects to the corpse.

First to arrive (within ten minutes of death) are common green flies that feed on flesh and lay their eggs in the mouth, nose and ears. Twelve hours later, the eggs hatch into maggots that feed on tissues.

After the maggots leave, beetles arrive to eat the drying skin. Later, other insects, such as spiders and millipedes arrive to eat on the corpse. These cycles of insects are so precise and fixed that forensic entomologists can establish a very accurate time of death.

Insect Detectives: Forensic Entomology

10 minutes	Ten minutes after body is dead in open air, flies arrive and lay thousands of eggs in the mouth, nose and eyes of the corpse.
12 hours	Eggs hatch and maggots feed on the tissues.
24-36 hours	Beetles arrive and feast on the dry skin.
48 hours	Spiders, mites and millipedes arrive to feed on the bugs that are there.

This determination is very accurate. The life cycles of the insects are so fixed and precise that they act as natural clocks. The bug behavior can indicate whether the victim was killed indoors or out, during the night or day, in warm or cold, in shade or sun.

Sequential Changes to the Body Following Death

The moment of death: The process of dying begins when the heart stops beating and no pulse is present. Breathing first becomes strained, intermittent, and after one or two minutes, stops altogether. There may be one last deep gurgling breath, called the "death rattle," that marks the onset of death. The skin becomes pale and taut, and all the muscles relax. Sphincters lose tone as muscles relax, and there is loss of bladder and bowel contents. The body rapidly begins to lose heat at the rate of 1½° Fahrenheit per hour. This varies depending on the environmental temperature.

After thirty minutes: The skin becomes purplish as blood sinks under the pull of gravity. The skin takes on a waxy, almost translucent look; lips and nails become pale. If the body is lying on its back, the blood collects along the back and on the underside of arms and legs. Any pressure on the skin will disperse blood at this area, making the skin white. The extremities will have turned blue. The eyes will have begun to flatten from loss of fluid.

After four hours: Rigor mortis (rigidity of the body) will become evident. Stiffening will occur first with very small muscles, first noticeable at the eyelids, face, lower jaw and neck before spreading to the rest of the body.

After rigor mortis has spread throughout the entire body and involved all the muscles, it will begin to disappear by the same route, involving small muscles first, then large muscle groups. After thirty hours, all the muscles will have relaxed again. The relaxation and "softening" of muscles is due to decomposition of the muscle fibers.

After twenty-four hours: The body will have cooled to the temperature of the environment. The skin of the head and neck now begins to turn greenish-red, and over the next few days the discoloration will spread to the chest, thighs and the entire body. Facial features become unrecognizable and the body begins to smell of rotting meat. Decomposition is accelerated by warm temperatures, slowed by cold temperatures.

After three days: Gas starts to form inside as bacteria dissolve tissues; this gas may form blisters 2 to 3 inches in diameter on the skin. The body may swell grossly, and may leak fluids from the orifices (nose, mouth, vagina).

After three weeks: The skin, hair and nails become loose and easy to pull off. The skin begins to burst open, exposing muscle and fat. In warm temperatures, the decomposing body will be reduced to a skeleton within only three to four weeks; in cold temperatures, it could take two months or longer.

This excerpt from an outstanding novel details the early changes of rigor mortis and body temperature, but also notes the difficulties encountered in determining the *exact* time of death:

> Fetching a long chemical thermometer from my bag, I took the temperature of the room, then of her body. The air was 71 degrees, her body 93.5. Time of death is more elusive than most people think. It can't be pinned down exactly unless the death was witnessed or the victim's Timex stopped ticking. But Lori Petersen had been dead no more than three hours. Her body had been cooling between one and two degrees per hour, and rigor had started in the small muscles.
>
> Patricia Cornwell, *Postmortem* (Avon)

Rigor mortis: Within a fairly wide range of variations, rigor is usually well established throughout the body within twelve hours after death and resolved after thirty hours. It usually is first observed in the jaw and neck, and appears to progress toward the feet.

Rigor mortis is due to a disappearance of the source of energy required for muscle contraction, ATP (adenosine triphosphate). When the ATP is completely gone (about four hours after death), the muscle becomes rigid and remains stiff until decomposition of the muscle occurs.

If there has been violent exertion shortly before death (such as a struggle with an attacker, a hanging with a struggle, or electrocution) the process of rigor mortis is speeded up because the ATP energy source is already depleted. If there has been death by carbon monoxide poisoning and thus, lack of any struggle, the process is delayed because a larger amount of ATP is still available.

A word of caution: Rigor mortis is one of the poorest gauges to estimate the time of death due to the large number of variables — activity at time of death, temperature of the environment and weight of the deceased. Extremely obese people may never develop rigor mortis, while skinny people develop it rapidly. Heat speeds up the process, cold restrains it.

Lividity (livor mortis): Lividity is a purplish "liver" discoloration (called livor) and is caused by stagnation of blood in the blood vessels and settlement into the dependent parts of the body. (That is, the part of the body facing upward is pale, the part facing the ground will be purplish.)

Fixed lividity means the livor (deep purple color where gravity has drawn blood to the underside of the body) can no longer be shifted by changing the position of the body. This occurs six to eight hours after death. If a body is discovered face down, but fixed lividity involves the dorsal aspect (the back), that means the body has been turned over, possibly even moved from another site.

When lividity first develops, if an investigator presses his finger firmly against the discolored dark skin, the pressure will cause "blanching." When pressure is released, the dark discoloration returns. After four to five hours, the blood becomes clotted and pressure will not cause blanching.

Temperature loss: If a body is warm, the person has been dead less than three hours; if cool to the touch, between four to six hours; and if cold and clammy, eighteen to twenty-four hours. Loss of warmth varies with environmental temperature, but averages a drop of 1½° per hour.

Changes of the eyes: Postmortem changes of the eyes are difficult to interpret. The cornea (clear part of the eye) becomes milky or cloudy within six to eight hours after death.

Here is a quick reference chart for setting up a scene or doing backstory. Remember, all of these changes are variable depending on environmental factors; most important is the temperature of the environment.

Summary of Postmortem Changes Over Time

30 minutes:	Skin has a waxy appearance, blue-gray color Lips and nails pale
3 hours:	Early nonfixed lividity (blanches with touch) Body warm to the touch No rigor mortis detected
4-6 hours:	Body cool to the touch Early rigor mortis in neck and jaw
6-8 hours:	Fixed lividity (no blanching with pressure)

	More advanced rigor mortis
	Corneas cloudy
12 hours:	Full body rigidity (body now totally "frozen")
18-24 hours:	Body cold and clammy to the touch
	Skin greenish-red
	Rigor mortis resolving, neck and jaw slack
30 hours:	Rigor mortis resolved, body flaccid
3 days:	Body swells as gas forms
	Blisters form on the skin
	Fluid leaks from orifices
3 weeks:	Skin, hair and nails become loose
	Skin begins to burst open

Here is how you might use this information in a scene where your detective quickly determines the time of death of a new client:

Sam Swift knocked again and checked the room number. It was the one the woman had given him, though she had sounded a lot classier than the smelly hallway he was standing in. He tried the knob. It was unlocked, but he soon discovered that his new client was no longer able to write checks.

Swift knelt down beside the young woman's body, careful to avoid the crimson pool that spread beneath her. He put his hand against the side of her face; it was cool to the touch. The muscles in her neck and jaw were already stiff where early rigor mortis had set in. The lower side of her face against the floor had a dark discoloration, and when he pressed his finger gently against her crimson cheek, it blanched pale. Swift let out a slow, deep breath. She hadn't made that phone call; she had been dead at least four to six hours.

THE AUTOPSY

Dr. Sally Rice, deputy coroner, adjusted the microphone attached to the front of her green surgical scrubs, snapped on a pair of sterile latex gloves, then picked up the chart and started to dictate. "This is Case Number 99-3760, Bobby Hicks. The body is that of a well-developed, well-nourished sixteen-year-old Caucasian male with brown hair and blue eyes. The body is 74 inches long and weighs 170 pounds." She put the chart down and moved beside the body.

X rays, multiple photographs, measurements and weight had all been obtained earlier. It was now time to proceed with the external examination and internal dissection of the body. Bright overhead lights blazed down onto the table.

"Rigor mortis is present in the extremities," the deputy coroner said. "The skin of normal texture; there is a single scar in the right lower quadrant of the abdomen from previous appendectomy."

She picked up a plastic ruler and held it against the chest. "There is a one cm gunshot entry wound on the right anterior chest wall with no burn or gunpowder residue present. There is a 32-gauge chest tube exiting from the mid-axillary line."

The autopsy was now under way on Bobby Hicks, who had been killed only sixteen hours earlier in a convenience store by a single .45-caliber round.

Category of Autopsies

Medical autopsy: A scientific postmortem examination of a dead body, performed to reveal the presence of pathological processes and to determine the cause of death.

Medical-legal autopsy: A specialized type of autopsy authorized or ordered by the proper legal authorities (usually the medical examiner) in cases of suspicious deaths, including suicide, homicide and unattended or unexpected sudden deaths in order to ensure justice for the purpose of determining the cause of death.

If a person dies without having been attended by a doctor in the past fourteen days, or under suspicious circumstances, or during a surgical operation, the coroner may rule that an autopsy is required. A medical-legal autopsy is required in all homicide cases.

Approximately 1 percent of the population in any given city dies each year; about one-fourth are investigated by the coroner's office. For example, in a city of 100,000 population, 1,000 people will die each year, and 250 will be reviewed or investigated.

A person brought to a hospital emergency room dead on arrival (DOA) is automatically reported as a coroner's or medical examiner's case. The coroner will investigate for possible foul play and determine if a complete postmortem examination is needed. All DOA cases will be initially investigated, but not all will automatically require an autopsy. Only those warranting further investigation or those suspected of foul play will have blood drawn for toxicology tests and to determine drug and alcohol levels.

This general category list shows the types of deaths usually investigated for cause of death:

- Murder
- Suicide
- Accident
- Sudden death in someone who seemed in good health
- Deaths under suspicious circumstances
- Prisoner or inmate who dies in custody

- Abortion (both legal and criminal)
- Deaths unattended by a physician
- Poisoning
- Death during/following medical procedures
- Before a body can be cremated or buried at sea
- A discovered body

Included here is a *complete* list of all reportable deaths that must be investigated by the coroner's office. This list is from the Coroner's Office in Lucas County, Ohio:

Reportable Deaths

All Homicidal Deaths
All Suicidal Deaths
Accidental Deaths
- Anesthetic accident (death on operating table, or prior to recovery from anesthesia)
- Blows or other forms of violence
- Burns and scalds
- Crushed beneath falling objects
- Drowning
- Explosion
- Exposure
- Fractures
- Fall
- Firearms
- Carbon monoxide poisoning
- Hanging
- Insolation (sunstroke)
- Poisoning (food, occupational)
- Suffocation (foreign object in throat) by bed clothing or other means
- Vehicular accidents
- Animal or insect bites (spiders)
- Therapeutic complications
- Airplane accidents

Abortions
- Criminal or self-induced

Deaths at Work
- All deaths at work, or work-related deaths
- Cassion (bends)
- Industrial infections (anthrax septicemia following wounds, including gas gangrene, tetanus)
- Silicosis, asbestosis
- Industrial poisoning
- Contusions, abrasions, fractures, burns

Sudden and Suspicious Deaths
When in apparent health or in any suspicious or unusual manner including:
- Alcoholism
- Sudden death on the street, at home, in public place, or at work
- Deaths under unknown circumstances whenever there are no witnesses
- Bodies found in the open, in shelter or at home alone.
- SIDS (sudden infant death syndrome)
- Death where abuse of the elderly is suspected
- Death of persons where the attending physician cannot be located, or death of persons which have not been attended by a physician within two (2) weeks prior to death
- All deaths occurring within twenty-four (24) hours of admission to a hospital unless the patient has been under the continuous care of a physician for a natural disease that is responsible for death.

To report a death, contact the Coroner's Office, or call the police and ask to speak to the coroner's investigator.

Not all cases that come to the attention of the coroner's office will necessarily require a full medical-legal autopsy. The particular case may only require a blood test for alcohol and drugs, or blood testing plus a superficial examination of the body before a cause of death can be determined.

When a case is brought to the coroner's attention for a ruling as to the cause of death, there are several options that the coroner or medical examiner can take, depending on the circumstances:

A. Make an immediate ruling based on the circumstance with no further examination.
   Example: An elderly person who lives alone is found dead in

bed. The coroner may rule "death from natural causes."

B. Take blood tests for alcohol and drugs, review the corpse, then make a ruling. (This type of limited exam would only be performed in rural areas of the country where a medical examiner is not available.)
Example: Victims of auto accidents, industrial accidents.

C. A limited autopsy, where only a portion of the body is dissected and examined before a ruling is made as to the cause of death. This may be done to accommodate certain religious restrictions, or the coroner may decide that only a particular part of the body needs to be examined.
Example: Industrial accident with a pipe through the brain.

D. Complete medical-legal autopsy for homicide, sudden death, suicide or cases requiring a ruling for legal purposes.

A medical-legal autopsy by a coroner is much more involved than a general autopsy performed in a hospital. It requires special training and skill, must provide adequate evidence for either defense or prosecution, and must differentiate "natural cause of death" from external causes.

A Medical-Legal Autopsy Includes:

- Identification of the body and tagging.
- Photography of body dressed and nude.
- Measuring, weighing and X raying the body.
- External examination of the body.
- Accurate detailed description of all wounds such as gunshot wounds, stab wounds or ligature bruises.
- Dissection and internal examination of the body.
- Toxicological examination of body fluids and organs (for evidence of drugs, poisons, alcohol, carbon monoxide).
- Opinion rendered, and the "cause of death" added to the Death Certificate.

After a death is determined to be a coroner's case, the body is sent to the morgue. The body is identified and photographed, then given

Sample toe tag.

an accession number. This number, along with the name of the deceased, is recorded on a tag which is tied to the big toe. The body is identified through family members, friends, dental records or fingerprints.

Needless to say, establishing proper identification is the first priority.

BODY IN CASKET HAS EXTRA LEG; FAMILY SUES

MIAMI—The family of a one-legged man whose body had to be dug up after it was learned a corpse with two legs was in his grave has sued the funeral home over the mix-up.

The funeral home "failed to check the toe tag of the body" when it collected a two-legged corpse at the medical examiner's office, according to the suit.

Instead, they accepted a "John Doe" body that went unclaimed for a month. A funeral home spokesperson said the medical examiner's office "gave us the wrong body."

After the mistake was discovered, the "John Doe" corpse had to be dug up and another funeral and burial held for the correct dead man.

Identifying corpses is not an easy task. Some are decomposed, some mutilated. When a body is left in the wild, maggots and animals devour it. Insects will finish off the last and leave a skeleton. In such cases, X rays of the body, dental X rays and bite molds may help establish an identity.

There are four specific things the autopsy should try to establish:

Cause of Death:	The instrument or physical agent that was used to bring about death (gun, knife, speeding car, poison, electrocution).
Mechanism of Death:	The pathological condition within the body that resulted in death (bleeding into the brain, torn heart muscle, lacerated liver).
Manner of Death:	The means of death. There are four possible manners of death: • natural • accident

	• suicide
	• homicide
Time of Death:	At best, the time of death can only be determined within a range of hours, and usually within days. (See chapter five on time of death.)

For example, the autopsy report for Bobby Hicks (see chapter two on the shooting and emergency treatment of Bobby Hicks) would state: "The cause of death was a .45-caliber gunshot wound to the chest. The mechanism of death was loss of blood and shock secondary to traumatic hemorrhage of the lung. The manner of death was homicide."

There are two things that an autopsy cannot determine with 100 percent certainty: the time of death and the manner of death. Both can be stated as an opinion with a degree of probability that depends on the available evidence and circumstances.

For example, if a man suffered a fatal heart attack during a robbery, the autopsy can only prove that the heart attack was the cause of death. The manner of death was in fact homicide, but without other evidence, the manner of death will be listed as "natural causes."

When a person is found dead inside a burned building, the question is whether the person was killed by the fire or was already dead when the fire started. Soot discovered in the windpipe at autopsy means a high carbon monoxide level in the lungs, and *that* means the person was alive and breathing when the fire started. The cause of death: smoke inhalation.

Determining the *manner of death* is difficult, and in areas of the country without a highly trained medical examiner, many cases are incorrectly determined. Sometimes there has been fatal violence without any external signs of trauma. Examples are: poisoning, **asphyxiation** by placing a pillow over the face, or a blow to the body or head with an internal bleed.

Other Information to Be Determined by the Autopsy

In addition to knowing what weapon was involved, the coroner should try to determine which wound was the fatal wound. If there are multiple stab or gunshot wounds, this may prove impossible.

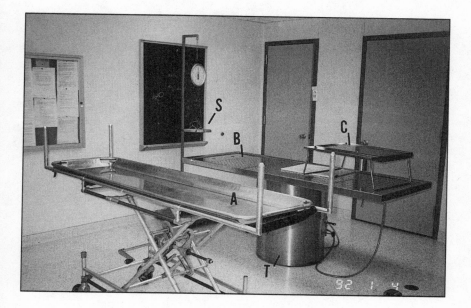

Autopsy room

A — Mobile cart for transporting the body to the morgue
B — Autopsy table with holes to allow water and fluids to drain
C — Small-parts dissection table with drains
S — Scale to weigh each organ
T — Tank for delivering water to the table and collecting fluids

In most suicides, the instrument of death will be nearby. But the absence of a weapon is not conclusive evidence that the death is a homicide. For example, if a person shoots or stabs himself and doesn't die immediately, he will have time either to dispose of the weapon or to travel some distance from it before he dies.

Questions the Autopsy Will Try to Answer

- What was the cause, mechanism and manner of death?
- What was the time of death?
- How long did the victim live after the assault?
- What weapon (if any) was involved in the death?
- Which was the fatal wound?
- Was the body dragged or dumped?
- From what direction did the injury occur?
- What was the position of the deceased?
- Is there evidence of sexual assault (rape or sodomy)?
- Was the victim under the influence of drugs or alcohol?
- Is there evidence of a struggle?

The Autopsy, Step by Step

External Examination of the Body

The coroner must carefully examine the body: first fully clothed, then naked. Blood stains, semen, glass particles, paint, powder or dirt on the victim's clothing may supply valuable information. The entire clothed and then naked body, including the injuries, must be photographed to document the findings.

It may be necessary to x-ray certain parts of the body (X rays of the skull to determine the presence of bone fragments, or of the chest to determine the bullet track). X rays can also determine the direction of blows to the head and body by the type of fractures, show bullets inside the body that have traveled far from the point of entry, reveal knives, needles and other embedded objects that may otherwise be overlooked.

Every external feature and mark should be noted, including scars, eye and hair color, height, weight, skin lesions, tattoos, moles, dental work, age and general condition of the body.

Hands and fingernails should be examined carefully for any foreign material such as blood, skin or clothing fibers that would indicate a violent struggle with the assailant. This material might provide evidence as to the identity of the killer.

Gunshot entry wounds are measured, the angle of entry determined, and the gun's distance from the body determined (see chapter seven on gunshot entry wounds). A near-contact wound (with the gun's barrel within 1 inch from the body) will cause a burn from the short flame that bursts from the barrel. A close-range shot (from 2 to 4 inches) will cause gunpowder soot that can easily be wiped away. An intermediate shot (from 12 to 16 inches) will cause carbon stippling or "tattooing" that is imbedded into the skin in a ring pattern around the bullet entrance wound (see illustration on page 102) and cannot be wiped away. At this range there will be no gunpowder residue. A long-range shot (greater than 16 inches) will only have the bullet hole wound, with no burn, gunpowder residue or stippling present.

Dissection and Internal Examination of the Body

The order of internal examination of the body is basically from top to bottom. First the neck, spine and chest are examined, then the abdomen, pelvic organs and genitalia. Finally, the head and brain are examined. The head is examined last in order to allow blood to drain from it to facilitate the examination.

The chest: First, the chest is examined for rib fractures. Then a thoracic-abdominal incision is made across the chest from shoulder to shoulder, crossing down over the breasts; then from the xyphoid process (lower tip of the sternum) a midline incision is extended down the entire length of the abdomen to the pubis. This is commonly referred to as a **"Y" incision** of the body.

Next, the ribs and cartilage are cut through to expose the heart and lungs. A sample of blood is taken from the heart after opening the pericardial sac to determine the blood type of the victim.

The heart, lungs, esophagus and trachea are removed **en bloc;** then each organ is weighed, its external surface examined, and then it is sliced into sections to evaluate the internal structure or damage. Any fluid in the thoracic pleural cavity is aspirated for analysis. Microscopic slides of tissue from the organs are prepared for examination of cellular changes.

The abdomen: The abdomen is examined in general, and any glar-

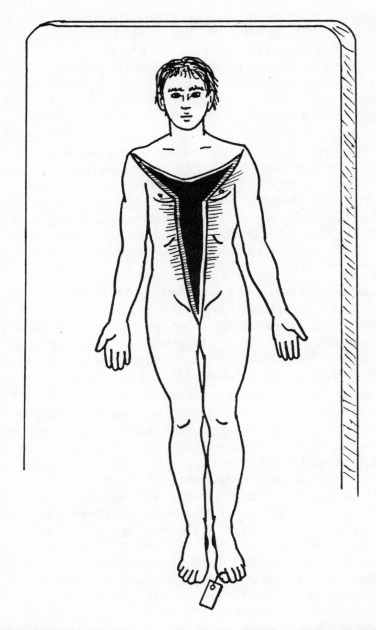

The "Y" Incision: The "Y" incision extends across the chest from shoulder to shoulder, then continues down the front of the abdomen to the pubis. All the internal organs are removed from top to bottom and examined.

ingly visible injuries are noted and traced before organs are removed. Fluids in the abdomen are aspirated for analysis. Each separate organ is then removed, weighed, grossly examined and sectioned. The stomach's contents are measured and recorded, with a sample sent for toxicology.

Usually the liver is removed first; then the spleen, the adrenals and kidneys (together); and finally the stomach, pancreas and intestines en bloc.

The pelvis: The genitalia are examined for evidence of injury or foreign matter. Vaginal swabs and anal swabs are obtained during the external part of the autopsy. In cases of fatal sexual attack (in which rape has occurred with murder), information useful in establishing the identity of the assailant, may be obtained by testing the seminal fluid found on the body or clothing of the victim.

Blood, semen and hair are collected and sent to the FBI lab or one of a few DNA labs for DNA typing. The DNA typing is *very* specific for one individual, and can be accurate for purposes of identifying the individual to greater than one-in-a-million.

After the urinary bladder is taken out, the urine is removed and sent for toxicology. Many drugs (such as salicylates, barbiturates and Valium) are excreted by the kidneys and will be concentrated in the bladder, making the urine in the bladder a convenient place to detect the presence of drugs.

The head: Finally, the head and brain are examined. The eyes and eyelids are examined for **petechiae** in the conjunctiva (the mucous membrane that lines the inside of the eyelids and the forepart of the eyeball). Petechiae are tiny hemorrhages in the form of dark red specks seen on the mucous membrane and may be caused by increased pressure in the head from strangling, choking or hanging.

The skull is examined for fractures, punctures or other injuries. Then an intermastoid incision is made across the top of the head. The incision through the scalp starts behind one ear at the mastoid region (see illustration) and extends across the top of the head to the back of the opposite ear. The scalp is then peeled forward and away to expose the skull. Using a saw, the top of the skull is sawed through and removed, exposing the brain. The brain is examined, then removed, weighed and sectioned for microscopic review.

I've included autopsy scenes here from several authors to show

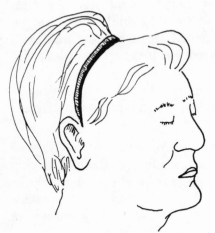

Examination of the Brain

1. First an intermastoid incision is made over the top of the skull, cutting all the way through the scalp down to the bone.

2. Then the scalp is pulled down over the front of the face, and the front quadrant of the skull is cut away and removed.

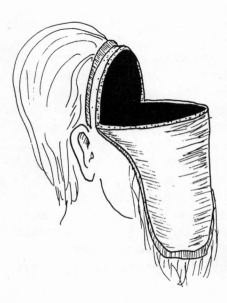

3. Then the brain is removed through the frontal craniotomy and examined.

how some of the terminology and details are incorporated into their scenes.

The huge "Y" incision that opens up the entire front of the body creates a very memorable, sometimes shocking sight to the nonprofessional and has often been described in literature. Here are a few excerpts from novels showing how these authors chose to describe the "Y" incision or the autopsy in general.

"Autopsy's going on now, but the evidence looks like suicide. No note, but an empty bottle of" — he looked back at his little notebook — "imipramine." His unpracticed tongue put the emphasis on the wrong syllable. "Mixed it with alcohol. Pretty lethal, I'm told, low LD-50."

Part of me heard his analysis of the amount of antidepressant Karen would have needed to ingest to have had a 50 percent chance of being consumed by a lethal dose, the LD-50. Mostly, I was transfixed by the image of Karen's beautiful body slit from chin to pudenda on a stainless-steel autopsy table somewhere across town.

Stephen White, *Privileged Information* (Viking)

One of the men moved around to the other side of the autopsy table and Ryan was looking at the whole body, cut open from breastbone to groin and seeing the man's insides, his vital organs and a slab of ribs, lying in a pile on the table.

Like dressing a deer.

The opened body seemed less human than the ones upstairs. It was a carcass with no face, or a face without features, a store mannequin. Ryan stared at the man's head and realized he was looking at the bare skull. The skin and hair had been peeled, pulled down, and lay inside-up over the man's face. That's why he seemed featureless. The attendant with the power saw had been cutting into the man's skull. He removed a wedge-shaped section. The brain was exposed for a few moments before the attendant pulled it out of the skull and placed it on the autopsy table.

Ryan, staring at the tag, let his gaze move up the yellowed legs, past the man's darker-shaded organ and thick pubic hair to the violent red opening. The assistant was doing something, scooping Robert Leary's stomach and internal organs into a clear plastic bag. He dropped the bag into the open cavity, working it in to make it fit, and laid the slab of ribs on top.

Elmore Leonard, *Unknown Man No. 89* (Avon Books)

I was making a Y incision on Cary Harper's body.

I removed the breastplate of ribs and lifted the block of organs out of the chest cavity while Marion looked on mutely. Water drummed in sinks, surgical instruments clattered and clicked, and across the suite a long blade rasped against a whet-stone as one of the morgue assistants sharpened a knife.

Patricia Cornwell, *Body of Evidence*
(Charles Scribner's Sons)

I described an autopsy in my novel, *Life Form*, by giving the reader a vivid description of the scene, then showing an internist's reluctance during an autopsy to face the death of his patient:

The autopsy room was cold. Like death. Air conditioning hummed from the ceiling. Torrents of icy air poured out of large vents onto the scene below.

Yost glimpsed at the waxy pale body; naked, lifeless-grey, and already completely gutted through one massive ventral in-cision extending from the top of the sternum to the pelvis. Chile's body gaped open to reveal an empty cavity. His lungs, heart, intestines, and liver had all been removed. Spine showed through the thin fascia in the back.

The casual manner in which this morbid ritual of death was being carried out made Yost uncomfortable. This was not his territory. He did not belong here.

Keith Wilson, M.D., *Life Form* (Berkley Publishing)

Issues Concerning the Cause of Death

It is important to determine the cause of death. Even for historical figures long dead, we have a peculiar fascination with knowing the *causes* of their deaths. In order to do this, a body must be exhumed (or disinterred).

Exhume: (v). To remove from a grave. The Latin derivation is from *ex*, meaning "out of," and *humus*, meaning "earth." A body can only be exhumed by authorities, such as police, court-appointed

Secrets From the Grave

Skull: The skull in males is thicker, heavier and has more prominent brow ridges. Older people have thinned, osteoporitic bones.

Face: The shape of facial bones can tell race and regional background. The teeth can tell age, general health and diet. In modern medicine, teeth are important for identification by means of dental records.

Arms and legs: The length of long bones indicates the height, weight, muscle development and kind of work or activity performed.

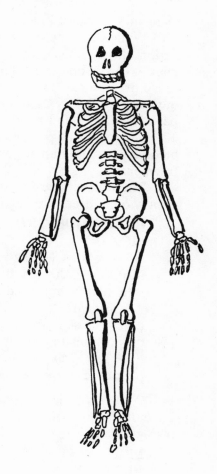

Nails and fingers: May contain DNA for genetic background and determination of blood type and presence of certain diseases. Bones in fingers and toes show arthritis, or give indication of repetitive activity or work during life.

Pelvis: A female pelvis is wider and lower. The pubis and sacrum tell whether she gave birth or not during life.

The spine can also indicate arthritis or wear from work such as carrying heavy loads. Bones of skull, ribs and pelvis may give clues to the cause of death of the individual (such as bullet holes, arrow or spear wounds, or blows to the head or chest with fractures).

individuals, or county government officials, and only by permission of the county authorities, usually through the coroner's office.

Dead men tell no lies—but they do leave clues. Forensic anthropology is the science that studies the remains of the dead for details of their past lives, as well as the cause of their death. By studying the bones, these scientists can tell age, sex, race and height. They can even tell the type of diet; vegetarians' bones contain more manganese, whereas meat-eaters have more zinc and copper.

While the body may have decomposed almost entirely, examination of the bones may provide clues to the cause of death. Head injuries can be determined by examining the skull, and fragments of tissue or bone can be analyzed for heavy-metal poisoning (arsenic, mercury, lead). DNA analysis also provides important details to the past. Bone, hair and nail fragments give DNA information on diseases, blood type, poisonings and genetic background. Even the blood types of mummies have been studied using the DNA of bone fragments.

The following article on the death of Amadeus Mozart more than two hundred years ago appeared in the *Tampa Tribune*:

HEAD INJURY, NOT FEVER, MAY HAVE KILLED MOZART
NEW YORK (UPI)—A new analysis of a skull believed to be Mozart's indicates the death of the composer may have stemmed from a head injury rather than rheumatic fever.

Mozart died on December 5, 1791. French scientists recovered a skull from a Viennese cemetery and studied it in all proportions to previous paintings.

The French team found a healed fracture on the left temple of the purported skull of Mozart.

And this article questioned the cause of death of President Zachary Taylor, who died July 9, 1850, just sixteen months after taking office:

PRESIDENT TAYLOR: WAS HE VICTIM OF POISON PLOT?
WASHINGTON—A coroner plans to open the crypt of President Zachary Taylor to test the controversial theory that he was assassinated with poisoned fruit more than 141 years ago because of his opposition to the spread of slavery.

An author believes she has uncovered evidence that Taylor did not die a natural death, as most historians believe, but was poisoned by arsenic.

The coroner hopes there is enough left of Taylor to examine. If Taylor did get a lethal dose of arsenic, his remains may be well preserved.

The results of tests on the exhumed body of President Taylor showed that he died of a stomach ailment and in fact was not poisoned. But the same day that the results of the tests on Taylor were announced, it was reported that the remains of Huey Long's assassin, Carl Weiss, would be dug up to determine if the young doctor was actually killed by Long's own guards. Long was a U.S. senator when he was killed at the age of forty-two.

Forensic scientists recently began looking into a famous murder case:

FORENSICS EXPERT LOOKS AT LIZZIE BORDEN CASE
FALL RIVER, Mass.—Almost a century after Lizzie Borden was accused in the ax murders of her parents, a forensics expert scanned their graves with radar Monday for clues in one of America's most celebrated mysteries.

Lizzie was acquitted in court but convicted in verse: "Lizzie Borden took an ax and gave her mother 40 whacks. When she saw what she had done, she gave her father 41."

If the skulls are there, scientists plan to exhume them, hoping modern science might shed light on the case.

Knowing the exact cause of death of those who have died remains a high priority in our culture. Maybe it is our need for a sense of order in life, or perhaps the occasional thought of our own death that haunts us.

Although we may be interested to know the cause of death in others, their loved ones may have a need for privacy. Consider both possibilities when you write such a scene. On one side, a detective is determined to discover the true cause of death in an elderly man; on the other side is his widow, who may wish to protect her husband's privacy and blocks the detective at every opportunity.

This unusual "Dear Abby" column appeared recently in the papers:

Dear Abby:

How lucky we are to be living in West Virginia. The newspapers here, as a matter of policy, do not publish the cause of death in their obituaries. I understand that in some states the cause of death is required. A friend who works at the local mortuary told me that a newspaper editor in another state refused to print an obituary unless "cause of death" was disclosed.

Abby, why would this information be important to the general public? The friends and relatives of the deceased know the cause of death without having it in the print for all the world to see.

N.J.G.

Dear N.J.G.:

The cause of death is not the business of the public, but some newspaper editors feel that no obituary is complete unless it is included.

When the cause of death is a suicide, some obituaries disclose the details: "suicide by hanging," "suffocation," "overdose," "shotgun to the head," "slashed wrists," etc.

Bless those sensitive editors who show compassion and report deaths without disclosing the facts that may have been painful to the survivors. The good Lord knows they have already suffered enough.

The Autopsy Protocol

The autopsy protocol is the legal document file presented in court for evidence. It is a folder containing results of the autopsy along with the opinion, photographs, toxicology test results, X rays and fingerprints. The report includes:

1. External Examination:
   a. description of clothing
   b. description and identification of the body
2. Evidence of Injury:
   a. external
   b. internal
3. Central Nervous System (head and brain)
4. Internal Examination of Chest, Abdomen and Pelvis

5. Toxicology Test Findings
6. Opinion

Opinion

The opinion comes at the end of the report and states the official cause of death. It is stated in simple terminology, giving the nature of injury, the cause of death, and any other factors.

A portion of Bobby Hicks's autopsy report is included here to show how a typical report is worded:

> The body is opened by the usual "Y" incision extending across the chest and continuing ventrally down to the pubis. The pericardium is opened and the heart is removed. Gross examination of the heart and review of sections through the heart show normal myocardium and coronary vessels. Over 1000 cc's of bloody pleural effusion are present in the right thorax, and a chest tube inside the chest is seen extending toward the apex. The inferior branch of the right main pulmonary artery is transected and the right lung near the hilum shows extensive parenchymal hemorrhage. There is extensive damage to the right lung along a bullet track, extending superiorly and laterally toward the right scapula. . . .

A long, detailed autopsy report would continue, including a complete systems review. The autopsy report would conclude with the *opinion*:

> *Opinion*: It is my opinion that Bobby Hicks, a sixteen-year-old male, died as a result of a gunshot wound to the chest. The bullet, a .45-caliber, passed through the right chest and avulsed the pulmonary artery, causing massive internal hemorrhage. The cause of death was a .45-caliber gunshot injury to the chest. The mechanism of death was loss of blood and shock secondary to traumatic hemorrhage of the lung. The manner of death was homicide.

Autopsies of the Fetus or Newborn Infant

As noted in chapter three, special rules apply to examination of a fetus or an infant that dies after delivery.

A. A fetus weighing 500 grams or less (less than 1.1 pounds) is considered nonviable. That is, even if it is alive for a brief period of time after delivery, it is considered medically nonviable. In this instance the fetus is considered a surgical specimen, and therefore no autopsy permit or death certificate is required. This varies according to state laws.

B. If the fetus weighs more than 500 grams and is born *dead*, then a special fetal death certificate is needed. The cause of death is prematurity and nonviability. No manner of death is ruled.

C. If the fetus weighs more than 500 grams and is born *alive* (even if only momentarily), and then dies, it must be registered as a live birth, and a regular death certificate filed. An autopsy is not mandated by law, however, and can only be performed after permission is obtained from parents or legal guardians.

If a pregnant mother is killed and the fetus weighs more than 500 grams, two death certificates must be issued: a regular death certificate for the mother and a second for the fetus. If the fetus is born alive (even if it lives for only a very brief period following the death of the mother), a regular death certificate will be issued. A fetus born dead will require a special fetal death certificate. (See also page 49.)

Summary of Medical-Legal Autopsy

1. Body arrives at the morgue.
2. Body is identified, assigned a number and toe-tagged.
3. Body is photographed and examined, both clothed and nude.
4. The body is weighed, measured and X-rayed.
5. Fingerprints are taken.
6. External examination is carefully performed:
   a. Clothing is thoroughly examined; fiber samples and stains are examined.
   b. Scars, wounds, tattoos, moles and other identifying markers are noted.
   c. Fingernails, hair and skin are examined. Skin of arms and legs is checked for needle marks.
   d. In females, a careful external examination of the genitals is performed to diagnose rape or sexual assault.
7. Fluids are withdrawn and toxicology tests performed.

Anatomical Nomenclature

Top:
is called *Cephalic* ("head")

Chest:
is called *Thoracic*

Side:
is called *Lateral*

Abdomen or
Stomach:
is called *Abdominal*

Back Side:
is called *Dorsal*
or *Posterior*

Front Side:
is called *Ventral*
or *Anterior*

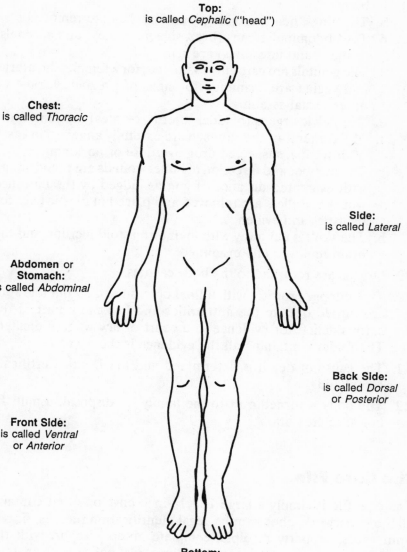

Bottom:
is called *Caudal* ("tail")

8. Dissection and Internal Examination performed:
   a. A body-length "Y" incision opens up the entire front of the body.
   b. The lungs, heart, esophagus and trachea are removed.
   c. The abdominal organs (liver, spleen, kidneys and adrenals, stomach and intestines) are removed.
   d. The genitals are carefully examined; for a female, the uterus and vagina are examined for signs of pregnancy, rape or other sexual assault.
   e. The pelvic organs (bladder, uterus, ovaries) are removed.
   f. The contents of the stomach are carefully analyzed in cases of drowning, suspected drug overdose or poisoning.
   g. The number and direction of bullet wounds are noted, along with estimated distance of gun as judged by the entrance wounds. Bullets are removed and placed in plastic bags for ballistics and evidence.
   h. The skull is cut away with an intermastoid incision and the brain removed and examined.
9. Organs are returned to the body cavities.
10. The autopsy protocol with a final opinion and all photographs are turned over to the authorities and become a part of the corpus delicti for evidence in a court of law when indicated. The folder containing all the evidence is the **case file**.
11. The cause of death is determined and the Death Certificate completed.
12. The body is turned over to the family for disposal, usually by burial or cremation.

The Case File

The case file is simply a large 12 × 14-inch envelope that contains all the paperwork, photographs, legal identification records, fingerprint cards, property receipts, complete autopsy report with the opinion, newspaper articles, medical records, police reports, telephone calls and other pertinent material that could be used in legal proceedings.

The preceding illustration lists specific terminology to describe position or location during examination and autopsy of the body.

This may be helpful to you as a writer when you wish to note something anatomically.

For example, a "ventral wound of the abdomen" is more accurate than "a hole in the front of the belly." However, whether or not to use the correct terminology depends on which character in your story is talking. A medical examiner might say a ventral wound to the abdomen, whereas a cigar-chewing detective might say "a hole in his gut." Read any of Elmore Leonard's books to see how he handles dialogue that varies according to the character speaking. The dialogue creates the character and brings them to life for the reader.

MURDER OR SUICIDE?

Our most primal urge may be the killer instinct. In nature, life feeds on death; with every creature either predator or prey. Nature, a testing ground for survival of the fittest, is a violent arena in which all must kill or be killed. This killer instinct once served a purpose to preserve self, status, territory, possessions, mates and food.

Humans may have started this journey as prey, but became predators in order to survive, and after thirty million years of evolution, have become the supreme predator. Our aggression grew out of necessity, but today, because that aggression remains in a world that we dominate, we finally prey on each other. Even in today's modern society, the mindless joy of the hunt and the lure of the kill are still a part of us. It is our past, our legacy. This anger, aggression, the impulse to strike or kill is ever present, whether against a stubborn soda machine, a VCR or a neighbor.

In nature, conflict is unavoidable; dominance and order regulate aggression. There are fights for mating and territory, but they usually are not fatal. With humans, however, conflict and aggression have no bounds. We kill not for preservation, but when pure aggression, as the primal urge to strike, raises its head.

Even docile people can become quickly violent: A wife kills her husband in a rage when she learns that he has been unfaithful; a man kills another out of jealousy over a woman; a middle-aged man who is fired from a life-long job, and is thus left with no future, walks into the factory and guns down his supervisor; a rancher kills his neighbor over a land dispute.

Violence, it seems, is part of our nature; no one is immune — we can all become killers.

These articles appeared in just one day's newspaper:

- **103 KILLED IN ATTACK ON NOMADIC SHEPHERDS**
- **FORMER HOSTAGE SHOT IN HEAD AND KILLED BY ROBBER**
- **CRAZED STUDENT IN IOWA KILLS FOUR, THEN HIMSELF**
- **ANGERED MAN DRIVES TRUCK THROUGH WINDOW AND KILLS 23**

"Battered Wife Syndrome Gets OK as Defense," the newspaper reported. On December 18, 1991, Governor Chiles of Florida signed a law that would allow the "battered wife syndrome" to be used as a legal defense for wives who kill abusive husbands.

The Manner of Death

Was It Murder or Suicide?

This chapter discusses in detail both the *manner* and the *mechanism* of death. Establishing the manner of death is one of the most important challenges facing the medical examiner. Because of an antiquated coroner system in many parts of the United States that allows anyone to run for the elected office of coroner regardless of training, there are individuals serving prison sentences for "homicides" that were suicides, while some murderers remain free because a homicide was wrongly interpreted as "accidental." Or a person may have died as a result of an accident, yet it was labeled a suicide, causing undue mental anguish to the family.

The manner of death can be established with reasonable certainty by knowing guidelines and probabilities. First, a quick review of terminology that was discussed in chapter three:

Cause of death: The instrument or physical agent that was used to bring about death (gun, knife, speeding car, poison, electrocution).

Mechanism of death: The pathological condition within the body that resulted in death (bleeding into the brain, torn heart muscle, lacerated liver).

Manner of death: The intent when a weapon or physical agent was used, and by whom. There are four possible manners of death:

- natural
- accident
- suicide
- homicide

This chapter will focus only on homicide and suicide. (See chapter nine on accidental deaths.)

Suicide

Suicide in Literature

Like murder, suicide is common in literature, television and movies. In *Anna Karenina*, Anna steps in front of a train, seeking to end her pain. In *Peach Tree Road* by Anne Siddons, Lucy kills herself. *Ordinary People, Dead Poets' Society, Sophie's Choice, An Officer and a Gentleman, The Great Gatsby, Interiors, Thelma and Louise* and *'Night, Mother*, just to mention a few, all have main characters who choose to end their lives.

Sometimes, it is the character's reaction to another's suicide that creates the tension and drives the plot. In the movie *Flatliners*, for example, Julia Roberts's character is haunted by the suicide of her father; this drives her to seek information about death, to see what it is like on the other side.

In the Pulitzer Prize-winning play (and movie) *Crimes of the Heart*, the story centers around the suicide of the mother who hanged herself, along with her cat. The youngest sister then tried to kill herself, first by hanging from a chandelier, then by gassing herself in the oven.

The suicide rate has increased steadily in the U.S. since 1950. It is highest among people 65 and older, but the greatest increase since the mid-1950s has been among teenagers and young adults. Males account for more than 75 percent of all suicides.

More Elderly Turn to Suicide

According to a new federal study by the Centers for Disease Control (CDC), suicide is especially on the rise among the elderly, and as our population gets older, the trend will continue to grow. Their motivation? They are alone, with failing health, and are terrified of what lies ahead. The CDC study challenges society to consider whether or not suicide is a rational choice for the elderly population.

Facts About Suicide

- More than 30,000 Americans commit suicide each year.
  - Men account for 24,000 and women for 6,000.
- Methods used for suicide:
  - Guns:

Men	64%
Women	40%

  - Poisons (usually pills):

Men	15%
Women	38%

  - Hanging:

Men	16%
Women	13%

  - Other:

Men	5%
Women	9%

Methods Used for Suicide

Shooting oneself is the most common method of suicide; next comes drug overdose. Although barbiturates were the most commonly used drugs for suicides in the 1960s and 70s, today, tricyclic antidepressants (such as elavil, travil or tofranil) are the most common. These drugs cause cardiac suppression, resulting in death from cardiovascular failure.

As will be discussed later, establishing the manner of death is a difficult task. Often it is impossible to know for certain if a death was suicide, and there are many times when only a reasonable probability can be made. This is one of the most important and difficult responsibilities of the medical examiner.

Cause of Death

This section will review in detail deaths from gunshot injury, drowning, strangulation, poisoning and stabbing. These five causes of death are the most common methods for homicide, suicide and accidental death. These are also common causes of death in literature.

This section will provide enough information for you to accurately write a scene involving suicide, homicide or accidental death.

Gunshot Injuries

History of guns in America: Guns played a central role in our nation's early history, beginning when the colonies first established a foothold on the continent, through the Revolutionary War, and finally the westward expansion. In fact, guns have been such an important part of our nation's history that the "right to bear arms" is guaranteed by the Second Amendment to the Bill of Rights, second only to "freedom of speech."

Amendments to the Constitution guarantee the fundamental rights and freedoms of every citizen. The Second Amendment states:

> A well-regulated militia being necessary to the security of a free State, the right of the people to keep and bear arms shall not be infringed.

Since the average American on the street no longer needs to "keep and bear arms" to keep our country free, other concerns face our society today. Guns were used in three-fourths of the homicides in the United States, versus less than one-fourth of those in other industrialized nations. Guns are also the most commonly used method of suicide in this country.

Americans own more than 3 million semiautomatic assault weapons, 140 million rifles and more than 60 million handguns. The nation's private arsenal is nearly big enough to supply a gun to every man, woman and child in the country.

America's passion for guns provides an easy way to vent that primal urge to kill. Homicide is the number-one manner of death for females in the workplace because of the number of females who work in all-night convenience stores.

According to the Centers for Disease Control, during 1984 and 1985, more than 62,900 people died of injuries inflicted by firearms in the United States. This exceeds the number of American casualties during our entire eight and one-half year involvement in the Vietnam conflict.

A report in *USA Today* of December 30, 1991, stated that more than 23,700 murders were committed in 1991, the bloodiest year yet, which set an all-time record. It stated that disputes among friends or family members remained the top cause, followed by drug trade and associated gang activity.

Firearms are used in three of every five murders. As crime and violence increase, the right to bear arms becomes more questionable. Some have termed the Second Amendment as "the right to die by firearms."

Bang! Bang!

At the moment of firing, here is what happens at the business end of the barrel:

1. First, a hot cloud of gas bursts from the barrel at the instant of the explosion of gunpowder. With direct contact of the barrel to the skin, the gases cause the skin to burst open in a "star-like" pattern.

2. Next, a flame (from burning gases and gunpowder) is present for an instant. At near-contact distance, this flame causes a burn-ring surrounding the bullet hole.

3. Then the bullet shoots out of the barrel along its trajectory.

4. Behind the bullet are projectile particles of gunpowder that are propelled for a short distance by the explosion. At intermediate distances, these particles blast into the skin causing "tattooing" that cannot be wiped off because the particles are embedded in the skin.

5. At close range is a soft cloud of soot particles from unburned carbon particles. This causes a dusky smudge around the bullet hole (at close range) that can be easily wiped off (as opposed to gunpowder tattooing, which cannot be wiped off). This soot cloud can also be found on the hand that fired the weapon and can be an important piece of evidence.

Discharge of a Firearm

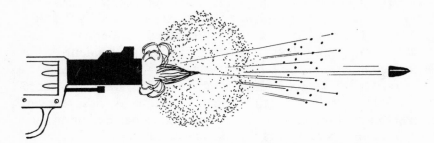

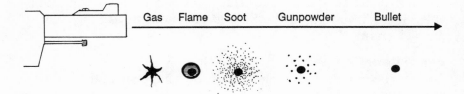

Events that occur during discharge of a gun and the corresponding findings at the entrance wound.

Summary of events occurring during discharge of gun:

Bullet	Round entrance wound.
Projectile gunpowder	Intermediate distance, causes tattooing embedded into skin.
Smoke soot	At close range, smudging that can be easily wiped off.
Flame	At very close near-contact range, causes a burn-ring around entrance wound.
Burst of hot gases	With contact of barrel to skin, there may be stellar bursting of the skin caused by gases ripping stretched skin.

There are several important elements to take into consideration when evaluating a gunshot injury. These are:

- Length of the barrel
- Caliber of the bullet (diameter in 1/100th inches)
- Type of bullet (shape, jacket, core)
- Distance between the barrel and the entrance wound
- Findings around the entrance wound
- Path of the bullet
- Type of exit wound

Examination of entrance wound for estimation of distance:
Tattooing, caused by projectile gunpowder embedded into the skin, cannot be wiped off. The distance for tattooing is short with snub-nosed guns, and longer for rifles (up to 3 feet). For most handguns, gunpowder tattooing extends out to a maximum of 24 inches from the muzzle (1½ to 2 feet). Newer types of powder load or longer gun barrels may leave tattooing up to a distance of 36 inches.

Soot, or gunpowder "smudging" (which can be easily wiped off the skin) is usually absent beyond 12 inches. Its presence indicates a near-contact wound. Gunpowder smudging and carbon tattooing into the skin will never be present at the same time; an important differentiation for estimating the gun's distance from the entrance wound.

For a star-burst splitting of the skin to occur, the barrel of the

Gunshot Entrance Wounds

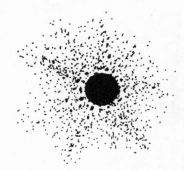

1. Near Contact
  (less than 1 inch):
There is a bullet hole and a rim of burn from the flame that is easily wiped away.

2. Close Range
  (1 to 3 inches):
There is a bullet hole and mostly soot around the wound that is easily wiped away.

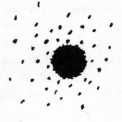

3. Intermediate Range
  (6 to 8 inches):
At this distance, there is no soot, but there are gunpowder particles imbedded into the skin with "tattooing" that cannot be wiped off.

4. Distant Shot
  (more than 15 to 18 inches):
A distant shot is defined as one at which no gunpowder reaches the target. There is no tattooing, soot smudge or burn; only the bullet entrance wound.

gun must be pressed against the skin with direct contact. The gases shoot under the skin, expand the skin and "rip" it apart by the explosion of expanding gas. This can only happen when the barrel is pressed against skin that is next to bone, such as the face and head, or the sternum of the chest. There is no space for the expanding gases because of bone, and the skin is stretched and "bursts" open in a ragged star pattern.

Thomas Harris describes the typical findings with a contact entrance wound against the sternum:

> Her breasts were small and between them, over the sternum, was the apparent cause of death, a ragged star-shaped wound a hand's breadth across.
>
> "What about the wound?"
>
> "I don't know," Starling said. "I would have said an exit wound, except that looks like part of an abrasion collar and a muzzle stamp at the top there."
>
> "Good, Starling. It's a contact entrance wound over the sternum. The explosion gases expand between the bone and the skin and blow out the star around the hole."
>
> Thomas Harris, The Silence of the Lambs
(St. Martin's Press)

The bullet's legacy: Three factors determine the extent of damage and injury to the body caused by a gunshot wound:

1. Caliber of the bullet (size)
2. Muzzle velocity (speed)
3. Design and shape of the bullet itself

Caliber: Bullets are measured by caliber, which is the diameter of the bullet in 1/100ths of an inch. A .22-caliber is 22/100ths of an inch across. Bullets vary from .22- to .60-caliber. Some gun manufacturers use the metric system; the diameter is measured in millimeters across such as a 9mm bullet (instead of using caliber).

With other things being equal, the larger the caliber of the bullet, the greater the extent of damage. Large caliber bullets can cause considerable damage to the chest and abdomen because of both the mass and velocity of the bullet. A .22-caliber bullet causes very little damage, compared to the tremendous tissue destruction and stopping power of a .45-caliber bullet.

Bullets

Bullets come in many different sizes and shapes, depending on the gun and the use for the particular bullet chosen.

Caliber: The caliber of the bullet is merely the diameter of the bullet in 1/100ths of an inch. That is, this .45-caliber slug to the left is 45/100ths of an inch in diameter.

In Europe, the bullet is measured in millimeters. For instance, an American .357-caliber is equivalent to a European 9mm slug.

Types

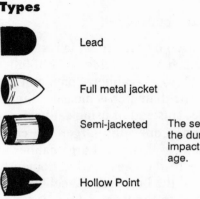

Lead

Full metal jacket

Semi-jacketed

Hollow Point

Dumdum

The semi-jacketed, the hollow point and the dumdum are all made to expand on impact and produce tremendous damage.

There are exceptions to this, however. A .22-caliber handgun is often used by the mob for a "hit" when the victim is shot in the head. The bullet will usually not create an exit wound because it lacks the velocity to penetrate the skull a second time; instead, it ricochets around inside the skull and causes considerable brain damage, hemorrhage and death.

Except for an execution-style shot to the head, it is unusual for a .22-caliber bullet to be fatal with a single shot to the body, but it can occur:

> It was another snowless afternoon in Aspen, Colorado, when French singer Claudine Longet shot and killed her ski-ace lover Vladimir "Spider" Sabich with a single .22-caliber shot to the abdomen. The small bullet transected Spider's aorta and he bled to death almost instantly. Longet's defense attorney argued that the .22-caliber "is the next step up from a BB gun."
>
> But the prosecuting attorney sneered in response, "Just a BB gun that cut the aorta and killed him, that's what it did."
>
> The defense that the caliber of the bullet meant that the gun was not a lethal weapon and therefore not dangerous under ordinary circumstances did not hold up in court. Longet was found guilty of reckless manslaughter.

Muzzle velocity: The muzzle velocity (the speed of the bullet as it exits the end of the barrel) varies from 600 feet/second to more than 5,000 feet/second. The greater the velocity, the greater the transfer of energy, and the greater the damage. A bullet stacks up tissue and produces a shock wave, pushing energy ahead of it, creating an exit wound far larger and more extensive than the small entrance wound. (Like pushing a snow shovel through the snow; as snow builds up, pressure increases).

A high-velocity bullet entering the skull causes "bursting" of the brain due to tremendous pressure as the energy of the bullet is expended. The high kinetic energy of a high-velocity bullet is transferred to the tissue within the confined rigid skull, and the head may literally "explode." A tumbling bullet (soft or hollow) releases its energy upon impact and causes much tissue damage at the entrance site. This is the opposite of a spinning full-metal jacket, which will have minimal damage at the entrance site and a large exit wound.

Design of the bullet: The bullet is the projectile part of a cartridge.

Bullets

Full metal jacketed bullets are designed to penetrate.

Lead, hollow point or semimetal jacketed bullets are designed to expand on contact.

Bullets are designed for specific purposes. There are lead bullets, which expand easily, but can be used only in .22-caliber guns because they cannot tolerate higher velocity loads.

Full metal jacketed bullets are designed to penetrate, and can be used with high-velocity loads.

Hollow points, dumdums, split-nosed and semimetal jacketed bullets can tolerate higher velocities, but are designed to expand on contact. These types of bullets have great stopping ability and cause tremendous internal injury.

The exit wound is always larger than the entrance wound because of a compressed wave of tissue and fragments that builds, like a shovel moving through snow, in volume and creates greater resistance.

There are three main types: a standard low-velocity lead bullet, a full metal jacket high-velocity bullet and a semijacketed bullet.

Lead bullets are made of lead alloyed with antimony, and are too soft for use with high velocities. Their softness allows distortion and flattening when they hit a target, and even at low velocities, the deformed and flattened lead can cause considerable damage. Most bullets are metal jacketed—usually with brass or copper. The soft lead core is covered by brass or a copper-plated steel jacket. Bullets with a full metal jacket keep their shape when they strike a target.

Expanding bullets—called "dumdums" — have a metal jacket in the middle and the bullet is open at both ends, so they flatten out and expand on contact with living tissue, producing great internal damage. All soft bullets, split-nose bullets, hollow-point bullets and jacketed bullets with the core exposed at the ends are of this type. They have tremendous stopping power, but they have been outlawed for use in war by The Hague Conference.

Teflon-coated "cop-killer" bullets are designed to pierce protective vests that are worn by law officers.

Accidental Shooting vs. Suicide

A single-action revolver can discharge just from being dropped, and thus accounts for most "accidental shootings." Semiautomatics and double-action revolvers will not discharge when dropped, but can be accidentally fired by pulling the trigger.

Factors used to determine homicide vs. suicide:

- Where on the body the injury occurred
  Most suicide shots are to the side of the head, through the mouth or into the front of the chest. Shots to the neck, the side of the body or the abdomen suggest homicide.

- Distance of gun from the body
  Most suicide shots are either contact or near-contact shots; with homicide, shots are usually from greater distances.

- Angle of the shot

- Number of shots fired
  One shot is most common with suicide, causing either instant death or unconsciousness and inability to fire more shots. Multiple shots suggest homicide.

- Presence of gunpowder residue on the victim's hand
  If the victim committed suicide, there must be some residue

of gunpowder on the hand that fired the gun.

- Other factors, notes or evidence at the scene
  A suicide note, evidence of drinking or known history of personal problems all tend to suggest suicide.
- Evidence of struggle or fight
  Evidence of a struggle suggests homicide.

At autopsy, the bullet is removed from the body (if still present) and packaged. This is necessary for ballistics to determine which gun fired the bullet.

When a bullet is fired, certain distinctive characteristics are imparted to the bullet by the gun. These markings can be examined and provide the investigator with certain general information regarding the type of weapon used. Ballistics evidence is found on the base and nose of the bullet, such as rifling marks from the barrel, which are distinctive for each gun, much like a fingerprint.

Bobby Hicks's autopsy examination of the anterior chest wall entrance wound revealed a 10 mm hole, 4 cm ring of tattooing, but no smudging. It was deducted from both the absence of soot smudging (which could have been cleaned off in the ER) and the presence and size of the tattooing, that the barrel of the handgun was 2 feet away from Bobby—too far to leave smudging.

Deductions from examining the entrance wound: Bobby was alive when shot, and the gun was approximately 2 feet away from him. He was deliberately shot at point-blank range. This important evidence shows intent to commit cold-blooded murder, not a shot that was fired during a desperate attempt to escape (which would have been fired from a greater distance).

The prosecution obtains a conviction of first-degree murder.

How fast does the person die? This varies according to the type of injury sustained, the type and caliber of the bullet, and which part of the body was struck. Can a cowboy die in the arms of his girlfriend as he whispers his undying love for her? Yep! You bet.

A bullet to the head can cause instant death, a type of execution used by the Chinese today. Or a person can survive hours to days, depending on the injury. People have been fatally shot, then run several blocks after their assailant before collapsing and dying.

Is there pain from a gunshot wound? With any kind of severe trauma (falls with broken bones, burns, gunshot injuries) there is usually a "grace period" that lasts from thirty minutes to an hour after the injury, during which the victim feels no pain due to the "shock" to the nervous system (see chapter two on pain after trauma). After this grace period, the person will experience considerable pain, often enough to send them into cardiovascular shock.

Soldiers have been known to continue fighting or to perform heroic deeds after sustaining massive injuries from gunfire or shrapnel, completely unaware of their often fatal injuries.

Does the force of the bullet spin a person around, slam them against the wall or lift the body from the ground for an instant? No. Even when shot with a large rifle, a person (or animal) will simply drop on the spot. A man I know took a direct hit in the thigh by a round from a Chinese rifle, one of the largest caliber rifles in the world, nearly amputating his leg. He said he heard the bullet, felt a blow (but no pain), and actually tried to walk, but fell immediately onto his mangled leg. The bullet, although a direct shot that hit him squarely in the thigh, did not throw him back or spin him around.

It makes a great scene in a movie, but in fact doesn't happen. Remember the scene I created with Bobby Hicks getting shot in the convenience store? I had Bobby thrown back against the wall, then slump to the floor. It is certainly more dramatic, but it is not factual.

If you are writing an action-packed adventure thriller, you may wish to slam your victims around; if you are writing a true-crime or are recounting an actual event (telling a war story, an actual police shootout or an assassination) you may wish to be more factual and less dramatic.

Depending on the area of body hit and the type of weapon used, you can make your wounded character have any range of disability following a gunshot wound, from limping away after taking a slug to the thigh, to dying from a shot to the heart or brain. But if you do have your character take two or three rounds—even if they are minor wounds and not fatal—do not have that person up and around the following day trying to track down a killer.

How can we use this information to set up a scene? Combine all the elements—entry wound, gun type and evidence at the scene—to create realistic and accurate clues for the reader. Here are two examples:

1. A person is found shot, no gun is found at the scene. The chest wall wound has no flame-burn, but does have wide tattooing

and wide smudging that wipes clean.

a. What kind of weapon was used?

b. Was it suicide or homicide?

Answer: Shot at close range with a snub-nosed revolver.

Reason: Close range because of gunpowder residue with smudging; snub-nosed revolver because of wide pattern of tattooing at a close range. It was homicide because a chest injury is not common for suicide; no weapon was found at the site; and there was no gunpowder residue on the victim's hands.

2. A hunter is found shot in the woods, and a question of suicide is considered. The chest wall wound shows moderate-sized tattooing, no smudging and no flame-burn. Gunpowder residue is found on his hands. A .30-30 rifle is found beside him.

a. Was it homicide or suicide?

Answer: Homicide, not suicide.

Reason: No smudging and moderate-sized tattooing places the end of the barrel of his gun two to three feet from himself. A rifle can't be held out far enough for the barrel to be almost 3 feet away; his arms couldn't hold it out this far. Someone else shot him with his own gun. Gunpowder smudges on his hands were from shots fired earlier.

Drowning

Definition of Drowning

Drowning: To die by suffocating in water or other liquids. **Suffocation** is the operative word in the definition of drowning. That is because there are two different types of drowning:

Wet drowning
- Accounts for 85 percent of all drownings.
- Is caused from aspiration of large volumes of water into the lungs.

Dry drowning
- Accounts for less than 15 percent of all drownings.
- Is a result of sudden laryngospasm (constriction and closure of the airway) caused by water in the throat.
- No water gets into the lungs.
- Laryngospasm cannot be demonstrated at autopsy.

Some Facts Regarding Drowning

- It cannot be proven by autopsy. Drowning is a diagnosis of *exclusion*, based on the circumstances of death.
- There are two distinct types of drowning: wet and dry.
- The amount of water inhaled can vary from almost none to large volumes.
- It is nearly impossible to determine the manner of death (i.e., accident, murder or suicide).
- A large majority of drowning is accidental and often involves the abuse of alcohol.
- Suicidal drowning is uncommon; homicidal drowning is very rare.
- After drowning, the victim's body sinks to the bottom and remains there until it bloats with gas, becomes buoyant and floats back to the surface days later (called a "floater").

The Drowning Episode

When someone sinks in water (or other fluids), the normal response is to hold the breath and try to get to the surface. When the lack of oxygen becomes severe enough, the drowning victim reaches a breaking point and has to breathe, taking water into the mouth and throat, usually inhaling large volumes of water into the lungs. The desperate victim continues fighting for air, taking in more water, gasping and struggling in a vicious cycle for several minutes until respiration stops. The lack of oxygen to the brain (cerebral anoxia) becomes irreversible, and death occurs.

Drowning is usually a slow, agonizing death manifested by a desperate struggle.

Establishing the Time of Drowning

When a person drowns, the body sinks to the bottom and assumes the position of head and extremities hanging down. When the body starts to decompose, gas forms within the tissues and the body gradually rises to the surface. When a dead body is found floating on the surface, it is sometimes referred to in the vernacular as a "floater." How long the body stays submerged (and for gas to form) depends on water temperature. In icy water, gas forms very slowly and the body may remain submerged for months; in tropical waters, this may happen in only a few days.

In cold winter water, it takes almost two months (sixty days) before the nails loosen from the fingers and toes. In warm summer water, this may happen within three days.

In drowning deaths, rigor mortis can develop rapidly, within two to three hours, because the violent struggling during drowning causes depletion of ATP from the muscles. (See chapter five regarding time of death and rigor mortis). Again, cold tends to retard rigor mortis, warmth speeds it up.

Here are some difficult questions that often arise when investigating a drowning:

- Was the victim dead before entering the water? That is, did someone kill the person and then try to make it look like a suicide; or did the victim die of natural causes, then fall into the water?

- Were any of the injuries, stab wounds or cuts on the body sustained before or after drowning? Was the cause of death in this instance drowning; or was it a homicidal stabbing or propellor wound injury? And more important, did it cause the death, or was it inflicted on an already drowned victim?

These questions present serious problems for the pathologist. Sometimes the answer is never really known. An opinion is formed based on the evidence, but often with little degree of certainty. Sometimes a swimmer will suffer a **stroke**, heart attack or epileptic seizure in the water, which may cause instant death (from natural causes); or may be so incapacitating that the victim drowns.

Was the Drowning a Murder, a Suicide or an Accident?

Suicide by drowning is rather uncommon, and it is very difficult to prove without other circumstances (suicide note). Death in the bathtub is frequently suicide. Often the person is under the influence of drugs or alcohol at the time of death.

With suicide in the bathtub, the victim is usually clothed; with a homicide, the deceased is naked, as the murderer tries to fake an "accident." A strong suspicion of homicide arises when a person is found drowned in shallow water. Homicidal drowning usually involves an already unconscious victim. If a healthy person is pushed into the water and drowns, there is no evidence to indicate foul play;

a dead or dying person may be thrown into the water to disguise the real cause of death.

Most drownings are accidental and are rarely a result of homicide. There is a high correlation between alcohol intoxication and accidental drowning. To prove homicide with drowning is almost impossible without other associated findings (evidence of a beating or struggle, cuts, gunshot wounds).

In a "Columbo" TV show, Lieutenant Columbo suspected that the killer had drowned his mistress in her bathtub, then removed her body from the tub and dropped it into the swimming pool to make it look like accidental drowning. Columbo was right in his assumption, but he was unable to prove it.

When the men from the police lab arrived, he told the medical examiner, "When you autopsy her, check her lungs for chlorine."

The medical examiner replied dryly, "Won't do you any good, Lieutenant. I can already tell you there won't be any evidence of it because chlorine dissipates almost immediately. And besides, couldn't tell anyway even if it were present because of the volume of pulmonary edema in the lungs."

Abrasions and cuts on the face do not necessarily mean that the wounds occurred before drowning. When a person drowns, the body always assumes a position of face down, with the arms, legs, and face dragging against the bottom. In streams or rivers with current, the face may scrape against the bottom, which forces weeds and sand into the nose and mouth, and this may cause abrasions of the face and forehead.

Material such as sand or weed found inside the lungs indicates that the person did in fact drown. If a person was killed and then dropped into the water to make it look like an accidental drowning, there would not be sand or weed within the lungs (but they may be present in the mouth and nose, forced in by the current as the body moves along the bottom).

Asphyxiation

Definition of Asphyxiation

Asphyxiation is death due to lack of oxygen. This is a general definition of a death that is caused by many conditions; it can conveniently be divided into three broad categories:

1. Suffocation: Death due to failure of oxygen to get to the brain.
   a. Drowning
   b. Smothering
   c. Choking (food blocking airway)
   d. Gases (methane, carbon dioxide, which displaces O_2 from the room). Carbon monoxide blocks uptake inside the body.

2. Strangulation: Closure of blood vessels and air passages of the neck.
   a. Hanging (suicide)
   b. Ligature strangulation (homicide or accident)

3. Chemical asphyxiation: Gases block oxygen at the cellular level inside the body and bring about death because oxygen is not released to the cells.
   a. Carbon monoxide
   b. Cyanide (gas chamber)
   c. Hydrogen Sulfide (H_2S) found in sewers and silos

Hanging

Accidental hanging is rare; homicidal hanging is very rare. Hanging is the second most common method of suicide and is usually done with a slipknot in a rope, belt or electric cord.

Most people who commit suicide by hanging drop from a chair or from a ladder and the result is that they choke to death slowly. The neck is rarely broken. It is common for there to be incomplete suspension, with the feet touching the ground. Hanging with the victim in a sitting or kneeling position is also common.

The rope will cause an inverted "V" bruise on the neck. The rope compresses the veins, but arterial flow continues, and pressure inside the head from blood causes small bleeding sites called petechiae that are present in the moist, soft mucosa of the lips, inside the mouth, and the lids of eyes. The face and neck are congested and dark red with either strangulation by ligature (murder) or with suicidal hanging.

In a judicial execution by hanging, the neck is broken and the spinal cord crushed by dislocated vertebrae (see chapter eight on execution by hanging). This is supposed to create an instantaneous and painless death (but rarely does). At least in theory, death is intended to be from a broken neck and crushed spinal cord, rather than from choking to death slowly.

In this passage, a detective is explaining to his partner what happens with a suicide hanging:

"A real hanging, you need a good drop," Monroe said. "Most of your hanging suicides, they get up on a chair, put the rope around their neck, and then jump off the chair. You don't hang that way, you suffocate. You need a good drop for a hanging."

"Regular hangman's knot up there," Monoghan said, looking up.

"The drop snaps the knot up against the back of the guy's neck, and it breaks his neck, that's what happens. But you need a good drop, six feet or more, otherwise the rope just suffocates the guy. You get a lot of amateurs trying to hang themselves, they just choke to death. Guy wants to kill himself, he ought to learn how to do it right."

Ed McBain, *Lightning* (Avon)

When a person is strangled or garroted, the bruise on the neck from the cord is a straight line, and there may be a bruise at the base of the neck caused by pressure of the murderer's hand. Almost all ligature strangulations are homicide, and most victims are female.

When there is strangulation by hand (or with a cord, scarf, rope) the vessels are occluded and the face and neck are congested and dark red. In most cases the murderer uses more force than is necessary to kill the victim, resulting in deep bruises, abrasions and contusions on the neck. With manual strangulation, there is squeezing and struggling, which causes damage to both the internal and external structures of the neck, often resulting in fractures of the hyoid bone (located at the base of the tongue) or thyroid cartilage.

Accidental ligature strangling is rare but does happen. Isadora Duncan, the famous dancer, died of accidental strangulation when the long scarf she was wearing became entangled in the wheel of her car. This type of strangulation may also occur in the workplace when a necktie or shirt gets caught in a piece of machinery.

Poisoning

Well, dear, for a gallon of elderberry wine, I take one teaspoonful of arsenic, and add a half a teaspoonful of strychnine, and then just a pinch of cyanide.

Joseph Kesserling, *Arsenic and Old Lace*

Suicidal Hanging

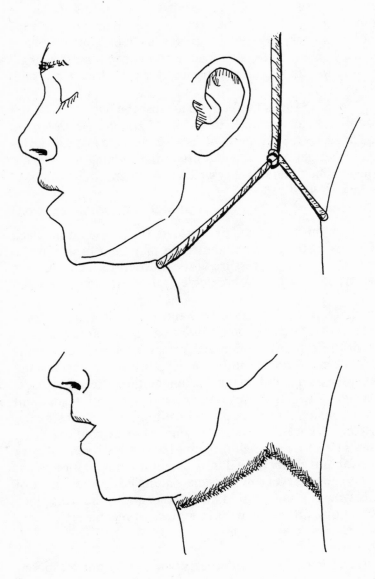

With suicidal hanging, there is a characteristic inverted "V" bruise on the neck, which corresponds to the rope pressure as depicted here.

Murder

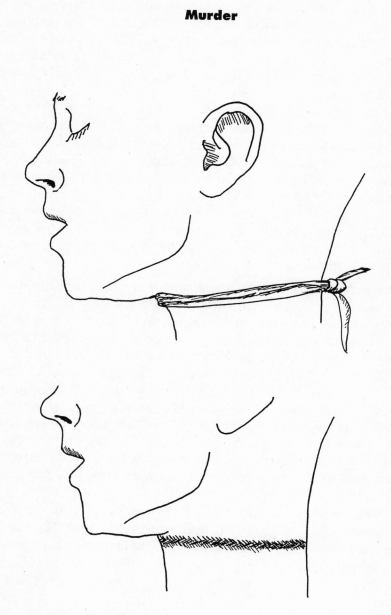

With murder, there is a straight-line bruise around the neck, which corresponds to the rope pressure as depicted here. There may be a bruise on the back of the neck where the murderer exerted pressure.

You probably never thought of poisoning as a form of asphyxiation, right? Well, that's exactly how cyanide and carbon monoxide kill—by asphyxiation. Although the subject of poisons was covered extensively in the book *Deadly Doses*, published by Writer's Digest Books, a short medical description of heavy-metal poisoning is appropriate here.

Poisoning has been a popular method of murder in literature, the play *Arsenic and Old Lace* being the classic. In *Hamlet*, poisoning provided the denouement, causing the deaths of both Hamlet and his mother. In the movie *DOA*, a man realizes he has been poisoned and has only twenty-four hours to live. During his last few hours alive, he sets out to find who his killer was.

Traditional homicidal poisons are arsenic, cyanide and strychnine. Arsenic is a heavy metal that is toxic to the digestive tract. Cyanide blocks the oxygen uptake by cells. Strychnine is a stimulant that affects the central nervous system.

Arsenic: Arsenic is a heavy metal, and is found in common items such as insecticides, rodenticides, pesticides, ceramics, glass and other products. In pure form, it is a gray metal, but usually is found as a white powder in the form of arsenic trioxide. It is odorless, tasteless and toxic to the gastrointestinal tract.

Symptoms include nausea, vomiting, colicky abdominal pain, diarrhea and dry mouth. The symptoms led Victorian physicians to term it "gastric fever." The victim may have a garlic odor to his breath. Other signs and symptoms include hair loss and numbness. Hemorrhage from the intestine and loss of fluids result in vascular collapse with dizziness, convulsions, coma and finally death. Arsenic is deposited in hair, fingernails and skin and can be detected years later in exhumed bodies.

Arsenic is only one of several heavy metals that cause poisoning; others include copper, gold, lead, mercury and zinc. Their common symptoms include gastrointestinal complaints of vomiting; abdominal pain and diarrhea; and central nervous system problems including fatigue, memory loss, tremors, stupor and eventually coma.

Cyanide poisoning: Cyanide is found in many industrial compounds, and occurs naturally in many common plant seeds and pits, including peach, apricot, apple and wild cherry.

Cyanide poisoning has been used extensively in literature; it has also been used in wartime, as a form of execution in the gas chamber, and as a common form of murder, as in 1983 when cyanide-laced Tylenol capsules caused the deaths of several innocent victims.

Hydrogen cyanide is a gas that prevents hemoglobin from bonding to oxygen and causes "internal asphyxia." After ingestion, reaction by the victim is the same as if a plastic bag were placed over the mouth. In this case a person can breathe, can move air into the lungs, but none of the oxygen is absorbed. There is immediate gasping for breath, and a desperate struggle as the person battles for oxygen that his body cannot use; he will gasp and wheeze while struggling for air. Choking, he will thrash about, sometimes screaming or sobbing. The asphyxiation is slow, and the victim strangles to death because the cyanide blocks air exchange, finally resulting in convulsions and death.

To verify the presence of cyanide in the body at autopsy, the body is examined under a hood to trap the fumes and allow the examiner to smell the cyanide. Cyanide has a bitter almond odor, also described as the odor of "dirty sweat socks." Not everybody has the ability to smell cyanide, and often one person in the coroner's office with the ability to smell it is called upon again and again.

Cyanide turns the blood and the tissues of the body cherry red.

Strychnine: Strychnine acts rapidly on the central nervous system, causing violent convulsions that result in death from sheer exhaustion and asphyxiation. Ingestion of strychnine produces very dramatic symptoms that cause the victim to jackknife back and forth in agony, followed by furious, savage convulsions. Because of the incredible energy expended by the body during the violent seizures, ATP (adenosine triphosphate, the fuel source) in the muscles is expended rapidly, resulting in an almost immediate onset of rigor mortis after death. The dead body remains in the convulsed position, eyes wide open and the face in an agonized grimace.

Carbon monoxide poisoning: Carbon monoxide (CO) is odorless, tasteless, colorless and nonirritating. It is less dense than air, so it rises to the top of the room. The most common sources of carbon monoxide (in order of incidence) are:

1. Fires
2. Automobile exhaust

3. Defective heaters

Carbon monoxide binds oxygen sites on hemoglobin and prevents oxygen from being absorbed. Its action is almost identical to that of cyanide; like cyanide, carbon monoxide poisoning turns the blood and tissues of the victim cherry red.

Symptoms include headache, weakness, fatigue, nausea, vomiting, collapse, then coma and death. The brain is the most sensitive organ, and early symptoms are headache, cortical blindness, memory deficit, hallucinations and slowed movements.

How to Tell Murder From Suicide

This section will summarize the differences between homicide and suicide, to be used as guidelines when you are writing a scene.

Gunshot Injury

Murder: *These factors suggest murder by gunshot*

- The gun may not be found near the body.
- Gun is fired at distances greater than 12 inches from the body.
- Shots through clothing.
- Shots through the eye, through the abdomen or from the back.
- Multiple shots.
- Evidence of a struggle.

Suicide: *These factors suggest suicide by gunshot*

- The presence of a suicide note.
- The gun found in the victim's grasp or near the body.
- Entry wound is usually contact or near-contact.
- In a suicide, the person will rarely shoot through clothing. If there is a shot to the chest (unusual site) then the shirt or blouse will be unbuttoned and opened.
- Usual entry site is to the temporal region of the side of the head or through the open mouth.
- There is usually only a single gunshot wound.

Drowning

Drowning is the most difficult manner of death to diagnose. There is no proven way of establishing the manner of death with drowning (murder, suicide or accidental drowning). Only a reasonable presumptive motive may be given; with drowning, death is usually ruled accidental.

Murder: *These factors suggest homicide by drowning*

- Drowning in shallow water.
- A nude body drowned in the bathtub suggests homicide or accident.
- Evidence of other injuries (bruises, gunshot, cuts).

Suicide: *These factors suggest suicide by drowning*

- A person committing suicide in the bathtub will usually be fully clothed since they don't wish to be found nude.
- The presence of a suicide note.
- Evidence of alcohol or drugs suggests either suicide or accidental drowning.

Stabbing

Murder: *These factors suggest homicide by stabbing*

- There may be "defensive" cuts on the dorsal side of the arms or palms of the hands as the victim tries to defend himself.
- Usually involves multiple wounds.
- Wounds to the side, back or stomach usually indicate homicide.
- The murder weapon (knife, scissors, letter opener) may not be present at the scene.
- Absence of the victim's fingerprints on the weapon.

Suicide: *These factors suggest suicide by stabbing*

- There are no defensive wounds on arms or hands.
- The murder weapon is usually at the scene, and the victim's fingerprints will be on it.
- There may be tentative "test" stabbings to see if it will hurt, or as the person tries to work up the courage to carry out the suicide.
- There may be additional cuts across the wrist.
- The presence of a suicide note.
- Stabbing is not usually done through clothing in a suicide; the

shirt or blouse is usually opened to expose the skin.

Hanging

The single most important factor in determining if a person hanged himself or was strangled is the shape of the bruise on the neck. If a person was unconscious and placed in a rope and allowed to hang, there is no way of proving the manner of death—that is, whether suicide or homicide.

Murder: *These factors suggest homicide by strangling*

- There is a straight-line bruise around the neck.
- There may be a bruise at the base of the neck posteriorly, caused by pressure from the killer's hand against the neck.

Suicide: *These factors suggest suicide by hanging*

- The bruise on the neck from the rope is an inverted "V."
- The presence of a suicide note.
- There is usually a chair or ladder nearby from which the person jumped.

CRIME AND PUNISHMENT

Death holds for most of us an allure that is quickly tempered by a strong aversion. It attracts us, yet at the same time, we shy away, repulsed, not wanting to get too close to it. This duality of human nature is what sells mystery and true-crime books. They chronicle the victims, the murderers, the punishment, the raw faces of death.

Every Western industrial nation except the United States has stopped executing criminals. In the U.S., however, we seem to be just as fascinated with execution as we are with murder.

This chapter outlines very graphic, detailed information on all types of capital punishment used in the United States at this time. I've included sections by Norman Mailer and Truman Capote to show you how they wrote their account of executions.

Public Executions

Public executions were prevalent in both England and the United States well into the nineteenth century. Hangings were performed in public and hundreds of people gathered in the square to watch the arrival of the condemned, the whole ordeal of the execution, and finally the removal of the corpse for burial.

The last public execution in the United States took place on May 21, 1937, when Roscoe Jackson was hanged in Galena, Missouri. But the controversy over public executions was reopened April 1991, when a television station in San Francisco sued for the right to broadcast the next execution in California's gas chamber.

Some people feared that it would create sympathy for the condemned, others feared that it would deprive the condemned's right to privacy for the last agonizing moments of life. A group called Death Penalty Focus announced support for television broadcast of the execution because, although opposed to executions, the group feels that if the public can see what executions are like, they also will oppose them.

In 1834, Pennsylvania banned public executions, and soon thereafter most states abolished the death penalty for a short time. Executions became common again during the Civil War, and continued until 1967, when only one person was executed. At that time public opinion was strongly against the death penalty. But by 1976, opinion shifted the other way, and the Supreme Court that year reinstated the death penalty as a deterrent to murder and other capital crimes.

Some opponents argue that only the poor and racial minorities are executed, and that wealthy people with influence are never executed. It also has not been shown to be an effective deterrent to murder; most people on death row claim they murdered without any thought of the consequences. When the first person was electrocuted in Florida in 1979 after a fifteen-year hiatus, the U.S. homicide rate increased 14 percent in the next six months.

Gary Gilmore, who was executed by firing squad in Utah, said, "Murder is just a thing of itself, a rage, and rage is not reason. . . . It vents a rage."

According to Carl Sifakis in *Encyclopedia of American Crime*, some individuals have committed murder only *because* the death penalty exists. An Oklahoma farmer shot to death a total stranger and told police, "I was tired of living." Another Oklahoma murderer strangled his cellmate so as to speed his own execution. Sifakis also reported that a man who helped build Missouri's gas chamber killed a young girl, then turned himself in, stating that his only motive for the killing was to be able to die in the gas chamber.

Regional influences are still the most powerful factor in death sentences and executions. The South has always favored the death penalty; 1,887 people were put to death in the South between 1935 and 1969. Here is a list of the states that have executed the most people since 1976 after the death penalty was reinstated by the Supreme Court:

STATE	NUMBER EXECUTED, AS OF 1991
Texas	40
Florida	27
Louisiana	19
Georgia	14
Virginia	11
Alabama	8
Mississippi	5
Nevada	5

Capital Punishment

The term *capital punishment* comes from the Latin word *caput*, meaning "head." (*Capita* is the plural). The original phrase literally meant "off with their heads." The methods to achieve that end were the sword, the axe and the guillotine. Some Middle Eastern countries still use public decapitation today.

Throughout history, kings, queens and commoners have been summarily decapitated. King Louis XVI, King Charles I of England, Marie Antoinette, Sir Walter Raleigh, Lady Jane, Mary Queen of Scots and scores of others lost their heads on the block. Anne Boleyn and Catherine Howard, wives of Henry VIII, fell to the axe. King Herod beheaded Saint John the Baptist and served his head on a platter as a gift to the maiden Salome.

You may think that decapitation has no place in modern fiction, but here is an excerpt from one of Tom Clancy's books:

The executions were at noon on Saturday, six days after the bomb exploded. The people gathered, Ghosn and Qati were led out into the market square. They were given time to pray.

Even though Qati knew it was coming, it didn't matter. As with so many things in life, it was all controlled by reflex. A soldier prodded his side with a sword, barely enough to break the skin. Instantly, Qati's back arched, his neck extended itself in an involuntary flinch. The Captain of the Saudi Special Forces already had his sword moving. He must have practiced, Jack realized a moment later, because the head was removed with a single stroke as deceptively powerful as a ballet master's.

Qati's head landed a meter or so away, and then the body flopped down, blood spraying from the severed vessels. He could see the arms and legs tightening against the restraints, but that, too, was mere reflex. The blood pumped out in a steady rhythm as Qati's heart continued to work, striving to preserve a life already departed. Finally that, too, stopped, and all that was left of Qati were separated parts and a dark stain on the ground.

"In all our countries," Ali said, "the sword is the symbol of justice. . . ."

Tom Clancy, *The Sum of All Fears* (Putnam)

Methods of Capital Punishment

Among the early colonists, there were reported cases of burning at the stake or being crushed by weights, but today executions in the United States are by one of five methods:

METHODS	NUMBER EXECUTED SINCE 1976:
Hanging	0
Electric chair	85
Gas chamber	4
Firing squad	1
Lethal injection	58

Hanging: It was the law of the old West, a horse thief hanging from a cottonwood at the edge of town. More than a few thousand people, both officially and unofficially, with and without trials, met their demise dangling from a noose made of hemp. Hanging is technically a very difficult execution to perform properly. It is crueler and more painful than other methods.

The sequence for a "clean" hanging is as follows. First the noose is adjusted over the condemned so that the knot is behind the left ear (and a black hood usually placed over his head so those witnessing the execution are spared the dying victim's final grimaces). His legs are tied together to prevent kicking. The signal is given, the trap door is sprung, and as he drops, the knot snaps behind the ear and knocks the person unconscious. The bones of the cervical vertebrae are broken, the spinal cord is crushed by bone fragments, and the body is paralyzed. Death comes in a few minutes.

Even with a "clean" hanging, the victim thrashes at the end of the rope for a few minutes. Wheezing can be heard as the victim struggles for air. A terrible stench follows as the dying person urinates, defecates and ejaculates simultaneously as muscle sphincters spasm and relax. After a few minutes, the dying victim's violent shudders stop and the rope stops dancing. There is usually one final jerk, then all motion ceases.

Below is Truman Capote's account of the execution of the two men convicted of the brutal cold-blooded murder of a family in Kansas:

The hangman coughed — impatiently lifted his cowboy hat and settled it again, a gesture somehow reminiscent of a turkey buzzard huffing, then smoothing its neck feathers — and Hickock, nudged by an attendant, mounted the scaffold steps. "The Lord giveth, the Lord taketh away. Blessed is the name of the Lord," the chaplain intoned, as the rain sound accelerated, as the noose was fitted, and as a delicate black mask was tied around the prisoner's eyes. "May the Lord have mercy on your soul." The trap door opened, and Hickock hung for all to see a full twenty minutes before the prison doctor at last said, "I pronounce this man dead."

While waiting for the second execution, a reporter and a guard conversed. The reporter said, "This your first hanging?"

"I seen Lee Andrews."

"This here's my first."

"Yeah. How'd you like it?"

The reporter pursed his lips. "Nobody in our office wanted the assignment. Me either. But it wasn't as bad as I thought it would be. Just like jumping off a diving board. Only with a rope around your neck."

"They don't feel nothing. Drop, snap, and that's it. They don't feel nothing."

"Are you sure? I was standing right close. I could hear him gasping for breath."

"Uh-huh, but he don't feel nothing. Wouldn't be humane if he did."

"Well. And I suppose they feed them a lot of pills. Sedatives."

"Hell, no. Against the rules."

Truman Capote, *In Cold Blood* (Signet)

In the following scene, Michael Crichton places the reader near the gallows, and with only a few well-chosen words, creates a vivid scene of the hanging of a young woman:

Pierce kept his gaze on the condemned woman. Emma Barnes was in her thirties, and looked vigorous enough. The firm lines and muscles of her neck were clearly visible through her open-necked dress. But her eyes were distant and glazed; she did not really seem to see anything. She took up her position and the city executioner turned to her, making slight adjustments, as if he were a seamstress positioning a dress-maker's dummy. Emma Barnes stared above the crowd. The rope was fitted to a chain around her neck.

The clergyman read loudly, keeping his eyes fixed on the Bible. The city executioner strapped the woman's legs together with a leather strap; this occasioned a good deal of fumbling beneath her skirts; the crowd made raucous comments.

Then the executioner stood and slipped a black hood over the woman's head. And then, at a signal, the trap opened with a wooden *crack*! that Pierce heard with startling distinctness; and the body fell, and caught, and hung instantly motionless.

"He's getting better at it," Agar said. The city executioner was known for botching executions, leaving the hanged prisoner to writhe and dangle for several minutes before he died. "Crowd won't like it."

Michael Crichton, *The Great Train Robbery* (Knopf)

And finally, here is one of the most sensitive and delicately handled hanging scenes I've ever read. I've included it to show you how a good writer provides specific details of exactly what occurs during hanging; the details are skillfully woven into the scene and the reader does not feel that he is being barraged with a list of facts. This is an excellent scene and beautifully written:

> His death was not instantaneous. Nor was it peaceful.
>
> This was not by design, for if the spinal cord is severed, a hanging will be instantly fatal. But the violent act was performed without skill, the noose improperly placed, and as a result the first three cervical vertebrae were not dislocated. Instead, three other factors contributed to his death. His windpipe was crushed, the blood flow to his brain was halted, and finally, the fragile nerve structures in his neck were ruptured. Death was lingering and painful.
>
> His body did not surrender willingly. Oxygen-starved cells, bursting blood vessels, limbs dancing in convulsive spasms, all his bone, muscle, and fluid screamed in silent fury. Beyond conscious thought, his frenzied instinct to survive fought its doomed battle against the darkness.
>
> Finally, death was demeaning. It occurred in a dark, forbidden place beneath the cold bars of a grill that had been used to anchor the rope. And when life had ended, the corpse's sphincters relaxed, soiling the body and its garments with the foul stench of death.
>
> It was a lonely and honorless death and was not worthy of the man.
>
> Anne LeClaire, *Every Mother's Son* (Bantam Books)

A *bad* hanging occurs when the rope is either too long or too short for the weight of the condemned to break the neck cleanly. In a "dirty" hanging with the rope too short (or for some reason the knot fails to break the neck), the condemned will strangle to death slowly, sometimes taking up to fifteen minutes. His wheezing is loud, and he usually jerks violently up and down on the rope while fighting for air. His legs, even while tied, kick out frantically for a hold. Death comes slowly, painfully and with great agony to everyone.

If the noose is poorly placed, the hard knot may gouge chunks of flesh from the face or head as it snaps, creating a gory mess.

If the rope is too long, instead of just breaking the neck, the violent jerk causes decapitation. Black Jack Ketchum was hanged in New Mexico in 1901, and after shouting, "Let her rip!" he hurtled into space and was decapitated.

In West Virginia, a heavyset wife-murderer was hanged with the same result; his body crashed to the floor followed by a thud as his decapitated head landed and rolled toward the witnesses.

Because hanging is messy and difficult to perform properly, most states have turned to other methods. Washington and Montana still utilize hanging, but also offer the option of lethal injection.

But there are countries where hanging is still used frequently. This article appeared in today's newspaper while I was working on this chapter:

28 EXECUTED IN IRAN

MASHHAD—28 people were executed by hanging in Mashhad, capital of Iran's Khorasan province. *The Islamic Republic News* said the executions brought the number of people hanged since March to 152.

Of those executed, the youngest was 21, and the oldest person executed was 61. Four women were among those hanged.

Firing squad: Currently the only two states to "offer" the firing squad are Utah and Idaho. When the execution is performed properly, death by firing squad is a very humane method. The condemned person is strapped to a chair and a small target placed directly over the heart. Twenty feet away are five sharpshooters armed with .30-caliber rifles, four with a single round and one with a blank so each person can rationalize that he did not do the killing. They take aim and, on command, fire in unison. If four bullets tear through the heart together, death is instantaneous and painless.

However, there can be problems. One or more of the marksmen may chicken out and aim away from the heart, knowing that his shot could not have been fatal since the condemned would die before the errant shot had any effect. Carl Sifakis reported a case that happened in 1951 when all four marksmen hit the man, but none through the heart, and the man bled to death slowly. While other countries use a coup-de-grace bullet to the side of the head immediately after the volley by the firing squad, this is not used in the United States. Because of the problems with execution by firing squad, most states have abandoned it.

On January 17, 1977, the execution of Gary Gilmore marked the return of capital punishment after the Supreme Court's ruling following a ten-year hiatus.

Long after daybreak, with only twelve minutes left on the clock, the Federal appeals court turned down his last stay. One of the guards said, "That's it, Gary, it's time to go," and with that, he was loaded into a van and driven to a site on the prison grounds where five marksmen waited behind a blind. Here is an account of the execution:

> Four men in red coats came up and put the hood on Gilmore's head. Nothing was said after that. Now the doctor was beside him, pinning a white circle on Gilmore's black shirt, and the doctor stepped back.
>
> Right through the cotton, Stanger heard the sound of heavy breathing and saw the barrels of the rifles projecting from the slits of the blind. He was shocked at how close those muzzles were to the victim. They sure didn't want to miss. Then it all got so quiet your attention was called to it. Right through the cotton, Ron heard these whispers, "One," and "Two," and they never got to say, "Three" before the guns went, "Bam. Bam. Bam." So loud it was terrifying.
>
> When it happened, Gary never raised a finger. Didn't quiver at all. After he was shot, his head went forward, but the strap held his head up, and then the right hand slowly rose in the air and slowly went down as if to say, "That did it, gentlemen."
>
> Schiller thought the movement was as delicate as the fingers of a pianist raising his hand before he puts it down on the keys. The blood started to flow through the black shirt and came out on the white pants and started to drop on the floor between Gary's legs, and the smell of gunpowder was everywhere.
>
> Norman Mailer, *The Executioner's Song* (Warner Books)

The firing squad is used frequently in fiction. Knowing specific details of how a real execution is carried out will help you write a more realistic and believable scene.

Here is a scene from Sidney Sheldon in which he ends the book by having the main character face the firing squad. It is an effective, powerful ploy:

> In her cell Noelle's hair was being coiffed when she heard a volley of thunder outside.
> "Is it going to rain?" she asked.
> The hairdresser looked at her strangely for a moment and saw that she really did not know what the sound was. "No," she said quietly, "it is going to be a beautiful day."
> And then Noelle knew.
> And she was next.
> ... The men led her to a post in front of a wall and fastened her hands behind her and tied her waist to the post ...
> ... She was filled with overwhelming sadness, as though she had lost something precious, and she knew that she had to concentrate very hard, but before she could see it, there was a sudden roaring sound and a thousand knives of agony tore into her flesh and her mind screamed, *No! Not yet!*
>
> Sidney Sheldon, *The Other Side of Midnight*
> (Warner Books)

The electric chair: The chair is usually of heavy oak, with a metal skull cap, thick leather straps to restrain the arms and legs, and a metal electrode on the leg. The prisoner's head is shaven to provide contact, and the path of the charge goes first through the brain; then the chest and heart; and then to the legs.

After the arms and legs are strapped down and the metal skull cap attached, all eyes turn to the clock on the wall. At exactly midnight, as the second hand sweeps past the hour, a switch is thrown and the first 2,500 volts surge through the heavy cables on the electrodes on the skull cap. Puffs of steam and smoke roll out from beneath the face mask, muscles jerk and arms strain at their heavy leather straps.

There are three separate charges; the initial surge is 2,500 volts, then the charge is lowered to the range of 500 to 1,000 volts. The first high-tension charge fries the brain, heating it to near boiling, coagulating protein, and turning delicate nerve cells into gelatinous clumps. The second low-tension charge is intended to disrupt the electrical circuit of the heart and make it stop beating.

The sudden surge of electricity causes the muscles to contract violently, sometimes causing bones in the fingers to snap. The heat generated causes the eyes to swell, so a leather band is placed over them to keep them from bursting.

Sparks, smoke and sometimes flames are produced as the body is turned into a high-tension line to complete the circuit. After the second or third charge has been applied, a prison physician will examine the condemned and pronounce him dead. The dead body is unstrapped, placed on a gurney and taken to the appropriate morgue for a medical-legal autopsy. There are black, deep charred burns on the scalp and ankles where the electricity ripped through the skin. Following the autopsy, the body is then released to the family for burial or cremation.

John Hill, reporting for Gannett News Service, was an eyewitness to a recent electrocution in Louisiana and gave this account:

> The execution chamber was bright spring-green. A straight-backed oak chair with eight heavy leather straps and a chin strap sat in the center. A guard brought out a leather hood containing an electrical plate.
>
> The prisoner frowned, sat down and watched the guards buckle the straps about his torso, legs and arms. He looked each witness in the eyes. He was impassive; he appeared resigned.
>
> His left pant leg was pulled up and another electrode attached. The hood was placed over his face.
>
> The warden gave the thumbs-up signal.
>
> Instantly the man's hands and fingers jerked closed. His stomach muscles contracted. His body arched against the straps. There were four distinct jolts of electricity. Smoke and sparks rose from the leg electrode on the first and third wave. But after its first violent contraction, his body showed no movement.

It was over within seventy seconds. An exhaust fan was turned on. The body's hands remained contracted. Twelve minutes after he entered the room, the man was pronounced dead.

But electrocutions are not without difficulty, and things do not always go as planned when using the electric chair. The electric chair at Starke Prison in Florida is referred to as "Old Sparky." There was a malfunction during a recent execution that resulted in an inmate's head catching fire. Florida is the only state that puts a bit in a man's mouth, an act that may have prevented that particular individual from screaming.

This article recounts a difficult electrocution in Virginia:

EXECUTION REQUIRES 2ND ELECTRIC JOLT

RICHMOND, Va. — Virginia corrections officials said yesterday they plan to use two cycles of electrical shocks in future executions, after it took an extra jolt to put a convicted murderer to death.

The killer executed in Virginia's electric chair had to be given a second dose of electricity when his heart kept beating after the initial jolts.

A doctor at Greensville Correctional Center in Jarratt, Va., checked the condemned with a stethoscope and determined that he was still alive after receiving the usual dose of 1725 volts for 10 seconds and 240 volts for 90 seconds.

The process was repeated and the convict was pronounced dead 13 minutes after the switch was first thrown.

The gas chamber: In the gray, foggy morning, a condemned convict is taken into a green octagonal chamber and strapped into a chair. After the door is slammed shut and sealed, sixteen one-ounce cyanide pellets are dropped into a bucket full of sulfuric acid. There is an almond-ammonia smell as hydrogen cyanide gas fills the room and the poor victim struggles, jerks against the restraints and chokes slowly to death, a process that is slow and can take ten minutes or more.

The victim strangles to death because the cyanide blocks air exchange. He battles for oxygen that his body cannot use; he will gasp and wheeze while struggling for air. Choking, he will thrash about, sometimes screaming or sobbing. The asphyxiation is slow: His face turns purple, his eyes bulge, he starts to drool and a swollen tongue hangs out.

This agonizing, grotesque and painful struggle is probably one of the most hideous types of execution still used. Witnesses have described it as the most vile and inhumane of all executions.

Lethal injection: With the Supreme Court's new ruling that opened the way to capital punishment, the public looked to modern technology for a more humane method of execution. The search resulted in lethal injection, but if drugs had not been chosen, death by lasers may have been selected.

The condemned prisoner is strapped to a gurney in the death chamber, then stares up at the ceiling as he waits for poison to drip into his veins. Saline is started and flows through the needle for fifteen minutes before the poisonous solution of sodium thiopental, pancuronium bromide and potassium chloride is turned on. After another five minutes, the prisoner is declared dead.

Texas, which uses lethal injection, leads the nation in the number of executions with more than forty.

Lethal injection, first introduced in 1888, was rejected then in favor of the more "humanitarian" electrocution. It was first legally adopted by Oklahoma in 1977, followed by Texas, New Mexico and Idaho all in the following year. Now twenty states have adopted lethal injection as an alternative mode of execution. Texas was the first state to use it, in 1982. By 1983, it was the second most popular method, after electrocution, but ahead of hanging, gassing and shooting. By 1984, lethal injections accounted for sixteen more deaths — thirteen in Texas, two in North Carolina and one in Nevada.

Some states offer a choice between lethal injection and their standard method of execution. But death by either electrocution or lethal injection is neither instantaneous nor painless.

Here is the account of the first lethal injection execution that was carried out in Texas in 1982 as reported in *Newsweek*:

> It was shortly after midnight and Charlie Brooks Jr. lay strapped to the white-sheeted gurney in a red-brick chamber at the state prison in Huntsville, Texas. In a different setting, he might have been an emergency-room patient, but the catheter that had been slipped into a vein in his arm was hardly meant to save his life.
>
> At 12:09 a.m. a lethal dose of sodium thiopental was added to the intravenous solution, followed by Pavulon and potassium chloride. At 12:16 a.m. Brooks was pronounced dead — the first person in the United States to be executed by injection.

But nobody knows how painless the execution was. Some witnesses later said that there were a series of apparently involuntary efforts to breathe, and a churning of his stomach muscles. Since the execution of Brooks, the solutions used have been refined, and death is hopefully swift and painless.

Watching an execution in Texas is like watching someone go to sleep. Lethal injection does "sanitize" the death penalty by bringing about a quick clean death with no unseemly mutilation or distortion of the body; it brings executions into the twentieth century.

Prior to injection of the lethal substance, the prisoner is sedated by oral or intramuscular injection of narcotic or barbiturate (morphine, cocaine, demerol). Then a lethal quantity of ultra-short-acting barbiturate is administered.

However, even lethal injection can still be a messy, complicated execution. In January 1992, a forty-year-old-man convicted of killing a police officer was executed by lethal injection in Arkansas.

His execution was delayed for almost an hour while medical workers tried to find a suitable vein for injecting the lethal solution. During that time, he was stuck at least eight times in futile attempts to get into a vein.

A situation like this can provide several possibilities for you as a writer. If you are writing a scene that requires that a character be executed, you may choose to do so using lethal injection.

You might take the point of view of the condemned prisoner, telling his thoughts while he watches in horror for over an hour while they try to find a way to invade his body and snuff out his life.

You might show the same scene from the point of view of a medical technician who struggles to find a vein, knowing that he is causing unnecessary misery for the convict, horrified that he might slip and cause a painful, agonizing death.

You might tell the story from the point of view of the warden who secretly opposes capital punishment, and who watches in horror the botched scene in front of him.

Americans are ambivalent about the death penalty. Many believe that crime is out of control, and they see the death penalty as some sort of solution, however flawed. On June 25, 1991, the Senate approved the death penalty for more than fifty federal crimes. And a crime bill before Congress would expand even more the use of the death penalty in the United States.

State Death Penalty
(As of December 1988)

State or jurisdiction	Capital offenses	Min. age	Persons on death row	Method of execution
Alabama	Murder during kidnapping, robbery, rape, sodomy, burglary, sexual assault, or arson; murder of peace officer, correctional officer, or public official; murder while under a life sentence; murder for pecuniary gain or contract murder; multiple murders; aircraft piracy; murder by a defendant with a previous murder conviction; murder of a witness to a crime	None	97	Electrocution
Alaska	. . .			
Arizona	First-degree murder	None	82	Lethal gas
Arkansas	Felony murder; arson causing death; intentional murder of a law enforcement officer, murder of a prison, jail, court or correctional personnel, or military personnel acting in line of duty; multiple murders; intentional murder of public officeholder or candidate; intentional murder while under life sentence; contract murder	15	27	Lethal injection
California	Treason; aggravated assault by a prisoner serving a life term; first-degree murder with special circumstances; train wrecking; perjury causing execution	18	229	Lethal gas
Colorado	First-degree murder; first-degree kidnapping with death of victim; felony murder	18	3	Lethal injection
Connecticut	Murder of a public safety or correctional officer; murder for pecuniary gain; murder in the course of a felony; murder by a defendant with a previous conviction for intentional murder; murder while under a life sentence; murder during a kidnapping; illegal sale of cocaine; methadone, or heroin to a person who dies from using these drugs; murder during first-degree sexual assault; multiple murders	18	1	Electrocution
Delaware	First-degree murder with aggravating circumstances	None	7	Lethal injection

State or jurisdiction	Capital offenses	Min. age	Persons on death row	Method of execution
Florida	First-degree murder	None	295	Electrocution
Georgia	Murder; kidnapping with bodily injury when the victim dies; aircraft hijacking; treason; kidnapping for ransom when the victim dies	17	91	Electrocution
Hawaii	...			
Idaho	First-degree murder; aggravated kidnapping	None	15	Lethal injection or firing squad
Illinois	Murder accompanied by at least one of eight aggravating factors	18	118	Lethal injection
Indiana	Murder, with aggravating circumstances	16	51	Electrocution
Iowa	...			
Kansas	...			
Kentucky	Aggravated murder; kidnapping when victim is killed	16	32	Electrocution
Louisiana	First-degree murder; treason	15	40	Electrocution
Maine	...			
Maryland	First-degree murder, either premeditated or during the commission of a felony	18	14	Lethal gas
Massachusetts	...			
Michigan	...			
Minnesota	...			
Mississippi	Capital murder includes murder of a peace officer or correctional officer, murder while under a life sentence, murder by bomb or explosive, contract murder, murder committed during specific felonies (rape, burglary, kidnapping, arson, robbery, sexual battery, unnatural intercourse with a child, nonconsensual unnatural intercourse), and murder of an elected official; capital rape is the forcible rape of a child under 14 years by a person 18 years or older; aircraft piracy	13	48	Lethal injection or lethal gas

State or jurisdiction	Capital offenses	Min. age	Persons on death row	Method of execution
Missouri	First-degree murder	14	68	Lethal injection or lethal gas
Montana	Deliberate homicide; aggravated kidnapping when victim or rescuer dies; attempted deliberate homicide, aggravated assault, or aggravated kidnapping by a state prison inmate with a prior conviction for deliberate homicide or who has been previously declared a persistent felony offender	None	7	Lethal injection or hanging
Nebraska	First-degree murder	18	13	Electrocution
Nevada	First-degree murder	16	44	Lethal injection
New Hampshire	Contract murder; murder of a law enforcement officer; murder of a kidnap victim; killing another after being sentenced to life imprisonment without parole	17	0	Lethal injection
New Jersey	Purposeful or knowing murder; contract murder	18	21	Lethal injection
New Mexico	First-degree murder; felony murder	None	2	Lethal injection
New York	. . .			
North Carolina	First-degree murder		80	Lethal injection or lethal gas
North Dakota	. . .			
Ohio	Assassination; contract murder; murder during escape; murder while in a correctional facility; murder after conviction of a prior purposeful killing or prior attempted murder; murder of a peace officer; murder arising from specified felonies (rape, kidnapping, arson, robbery, burglary); murder of a witness to prevent testimony in a criminal proceeding or in retaliation	18	88	Electrocution
Oklahoma	Murder with malice aforethought; murder arising from specified felonies (forcible rape, robbery with a dangerous weapon, kidnapping, escape from lawful custody, first-degree burglary, arson); murder when the victim is a child who has been injured, tortured or maimed	None	92	Lethal injection

State or jurisdiction	Capital offenses	Min. age	Persons on death row	Method of execution
Oregon	Aggravated murder	18	15	Lethal injection
Pennsylvania	First-degree murder	None	98	Electrocution
Rhode Island	...			
South Carolina	Murder with statutory aggravating circumstances	None	36	Electrocution
South Dakota	First-degree murder; kidnapping with gross permanent physical injury inflicted on the victim; felony murder	None	0	Lethal injection
Tennessee	First-degree murder	18	70	Electrocution
Texas	Murder of a public safety officer, fireman, or correctional employee; murder during the commission of specified felonies (kidnapping, burglary, robbery, aggravated rape, arson); murder for remuneration; multiple murders; murder during prison escape; murder by a state prison inmate	17	284	Lethal injection
Utah	First-degree murder; aggravated assault by prisoners involving serious bodily injury	14	8	Lethal injection or firing squad
Vermont	Murder of a police officer or correctional officer; kidnapping for ransom	None	0	Electrocution
Virginia	Murder during the commission of specified felonies (abduction, armed robbery, rape); contract murder; murder by a prisoner while in custody; murder of a law enforcement officer; multiple murders; murder of a child under 12 years old during an abduction	15	39	Electrocution
Washington	Aggravated first-degree premeditated murder	None	7	Lethal injection or hanging
West Virginia	...			
Wisconsin	...			
Wyoming	First-degree murder including felony murder	None	2	Lethal injection
Dist. of Columbia	...			

PART III

CAUSES OF DEATH

ACCIDENTS

Use of Accidental Death in Literature

Death, because it is central to the human experience, plays a major role in all forms of literature, mainstream as well as murder mysteries, westerns, romance and spy thrillers. But there are more ways to use death in a plot than murder.

Accidents are a fact of life (and death). More than forty-five thousand people die annually in auto accidents in the United States. Accidents are the fourth leading cause of death for all ages, and the leading cause of death for everyone under the age of forty-four. For those fifteen to twenty-four years of age, accidents account for more deaths than all other causes combined. Over twenty-four thousand children die each year in the United States from trauma.

It follows then that accidents are prevalent in literature. It is often better to "kill" a character in a story by using the vicissitudes of fate rather than murder. These accidental deaths in literature are powerful tools, creating strong emotions in the reader, fertile plot trajectories and rich new conflicts for the survivors.

In *Gone With the Wind*, a horse fell on Scarlett O'Hara's daughter, Bonnie, and killed her. And Scarlett's father died when he fell from a horse when attempting to jump a fence.

Thornton Wilder's Pulitzer Prize-winning novel *The Bridge of San Luis Rey* details the tragic fate of five travelers hurled to their deaths when a bridge they were crossing collapsed into a canyon.

In *Centennial*, Elly, the young wife of Levi Zendt, was bitten on the neck by a rattlesnake and died almost instantly:

> Elly was up early to prepare breakfast. She did not heed the warning sound, and as she stooped to lift a large chip, a giant rattlesnake, bigger around than her arm, struck with terrifying speed and sank its fangs deep into her throat. Within minutes she was dead.

In *The Thornbirds*, Paddy Cleary died when a burning tree fell on him. His son, Stuart Cleary, was crushed to death when a mortally wounded wild boar fell on him. And Meggie's son, Dane, drowned while trying to save two women.

The movie *Stand By Me* is about four boys on a quest to find the body of another boy who was killed by a train.

In the biographical story *Lawrence of Arabia*, Lawrence had two servant boys. One fell into dry quicksand and died; the second died when a detonating charge exploded prematurely; and finally, Lawrence himself died in a motorcycle accident.

The preceding examples show how accidental deaths can enrich the plot, complicate the story, add conflict or move the story in a different direction. But sometimes an accidental death is *the* pivotal part of the plot or the event that brings about the denouement.

In *The Great Gatsby*, Myrtle Wilson, wife of the shabby garage owner George Wilson, and also mistress to Tom Buchanan, is hit by Buchanan's speeding car. Her violent, tragic death leads to a confrontation between Gatsby and George, ending with the murder of Gatsby and the suicide of George.

In Steinbeck's *Of Mice and Men*, pitiful Lennie Small, a giant of a man with enormous strength but slow wit, accidently kills Curley's wife by holding so tightly he breaks her neck. This leads to

Lennie's murder when his friend George shoots Lennie in the back of the head as an act of mercy, to protect his friend from Curley's revenge.

In *Anna Karenina*, Anna sees a man crushed under a train at the station. The episode deeply troubles her, and at the end, she herself chooses to leap under the wheels of an oncoming train when she decides to end her own life. The accident at the station set the stage for her own violent death.

In your story, be original and innovative when planning an accident for one of your characters or when you select a weapon to murder them. In the game *Clue* (by Parker Bros.), "It was done in the library with a rope, a lead pipe, a wrench or a candlestick . . . ." Many authors use these same old standard weapons, never inventing something new or different. By thinking up new kinds of weapons, you can create a newer approach to murder and perhaps a way for accidents to happen.

Here are some examples, both from real-life accounts and fiction that will illustrate what I mean. As you read through these, try to think of new, unusual means of accidental death or unusual things that may be used as weapons.

According to the *Hartford Courant* Lance Grangruth accidently shot a nail into his brain while working with a nail gun. He didn't realize it had happened until he tried to take his hat off and discovered it was nailed to his head. "I tried to take my hat off and it wouldn't come off." He also noted, "I've had worse headaches."

Pretty farfetched? Well, not exactly. In *Lethal Weapon II*, Lieutenant Murtaugh (played by Danny Glover) fights his way out of an ambush at his house using a nail gun. Using an unusual weapon, in this case a nail gun, makes the scene different and memorable.

Accidental Deaths Recounted in the Newspaper

Be creative and open to new kinds of "accidents" and weapons. Read the paper to get fresh ideas. Here are a few that I have come across, as well as a few facts and statistics regarding accidents that you might consider in your story. They may seem ridiculous or absurd, but that is the point: Every day, people die from bizarre circumstances; the accidents listed below actually happened and are presented to give you ideas for your plots:

WOMAN DIES AFTER BEING DRAGGED BY CAR

SEMINOLE, Fla. — A 73-year-old woman who fell underneath her moving car and was dragged around in a circle Monday morning died Monday evening, the Sheriff's Office said.

She left the car running, and when she got out, it started rolling backward. She fell underneath the station wagon, which dragged her around in a circle before hitting a palm tree.

MAN KILLED IN A DRYER

BOSTON — A commercial laundry worker was killed when he was apparently knocked into a huge dryer by 100 pounds of wet clothing.

He was preparing to clean the dryer when a pile of wet laundry came down a shuttle belt and knocked him inside, police said. He was trapped in the dryer six minutes.

SNAKE KILLS MOTHER, SWALLOWS CHILD

JAKARTA, INDONESIA — A python killed a 30-year-old woman and swallowed her 5-year-old child in a remote mountain village, a newspaper reported Friday.

The newspaper said the dead woman was found after the 18-foot-long snake attacked her and her baby in Ranapanjang, a village 250 miles northwest of Jakarta.

GARBAGE TRUCK ALMOST KILLS MAN IN DUMPSTER

CLEARWATER — A man slept in a dumpster because he felt safe there — but Thursday morning it almost killed him.

Only his frantically waving hand saved him from being crushed to death when the dumpster was emptied into a garbage truck and its compactor activated.

A sanitation worker saw the man's hand over the edge of the steel wall, and turned off the compactor. It stopped only inches from him.

"If my backup man hadn't spotted him, I would have compacted him," the worker said.

"It was terrible," the man said. "I woke up to find myself inches from being crushed to death. That makes sleep difficult."

MOTORCYCLIST DIES AFTER BIKE GETS BLESSING

LITCHFIELD — Hundreds of motorcyclists got their bikes blessed at the Our Lady of Lourdes Shrine, hoping the rite would protect them in their travels.

But one 67-year-old man never got to take his next ride.

While kick-starting his Harley-Davidson minutes after the 13th annual blessing, the man suffered a heart attack and fell to the ground.

The man had tried to kick-start his motorcycle for three to four minutes before he fell dead.

The priest giving the blessings then gave him the last rites.

76-YEAR OLD PATIENT DIES AFTER STRETCHER OVERTURNS

PITTSBURGH — A 76-year-old man died after the ambulance stretcher he was strapped to rolled down a grade and overturned, the coroner's office said. He was being transported from a nursing home to a doctor's office for an appointment. The ambulance attendants left the stretcher in the parking lot. The cot rolled away and turned over, killing the man.

SHOPPING-CART HAZARD

The next time you take a youngster food-shopping, consider this: in 1989 more than 12,000 children under the age of 5 were treated in hospital emergency rooms for head injuries resulting from shopping-cart accidents, the Consumer Product Safety Commission said. Most injuries were due to falls from the carts, and one-third were concussions, fractures, or internal injuries. Use seat belts when they are available and watch your children closely.

SAILOR FALLS INTO VOLCANO CRATER

HAWAII — A sailor hiking at the summit of Kilauea Volcano in Hawaii plunged to his death in the volcano's crater, an official said Saturday.

The 23-year-old man was hiking with three other Navy men when he walked over the rim and fell down the 400-foot slope, said the chief ranger at Hawaii Volcanoes National Park.

BACKBOARD FALLS, KILLS BASKETBALL PLAYER

COLUMBUS — A man died yesterday from head injuries suffered when a basketball backboard fell on him, authorities said. The deputy coroner said the man was playing basketball Monday afternoon with friends when the backboard crashed down on his head. He apparently jammed the ball through the net and as he was coming down, the backboard came down with him.

Danger From Insects

Arachnophobia!

L.A. SPOOKED BY SOUTH AMERICAN SPIDER

LOS ANGELES — A new wave of illegal immigrants has tangled the city in a web of intrigue.

How did a rare and potentially lethal species of spiders weave their way up from their native South America into downtown L.A. buildings?

A bite from the violin spider, which gets its name from the violin-shaped pattern on its back, can be deadly if not treated immediately. The venom destroys the tissues and leaves an ugly scar. "You think you're falling apart," the head of the county Vectorborne Disease Surveillance Program said.

The Brown Recluse Spider

Most spiders are venomous but timid and are seldom capable of penetrating the skin. But brown recluse spiders are more aggressive and toxic. They are commonly found in out-buildings and storage areas (called "recluse" because of this). They are called "fiddle-backed" because of a violin shape on their back. The very dangerous South American brown spider has become prevalent in Southern California. The bite can cause **necrosis** of heart and kidney tissue, and a breakdown of red blood cells with **hemolytic** reactions. Convulsions and death may result.

Black Widow Spider

This is the classic "killer spider," appearing often in both literature and movies. Redness and swelling appear around the bite and there is an immediate pinprick sensation. Anxiety, nausea, vomiting, dizziness, headache, shortness of breath, edema of the eyelids and skin rash are common. Fatalities from black widow bites are usually seen only in young children and in the very old.

Fire Ants

TINY FIRE ANT PACKS FIERCE PAIN, SUFFERING IN ITS MOUTH

WEST PALM BEACH — All it took was a tiny red ant to send a young woman to the hospital. The attack — the most recent of five in five years — could have killed her.

In recent years the sting of the fire ant has killed 22 people in Florida, more than in any of the 11 Southeast states that have the menacing devils.

"It takes exquisitely small amounts of exposure to produce an extreme allergic reaction," said one doctor. Two of his patients have died from fire-ant stings.

Fire ants average 5 mm in length and may be red, brown or black. They are aggressive inhabitants of agricultural areas and attack humans or livestock in swarms.

The fire ant is believed to have been imported from Brazil fifty years ago aboard a cargo ship. Today, the ants infest 280 million acres in the southeast United States, including 30 million acres in Florida.

They build mounds up to 3 feet high and 4 feet across that can hold populations of 250,000. As many as forty mounds have been found in suburban backyards, with Ocala horse pastures having up to two hundred mounds per acre.

Other Dangers in Nature

Recently there have been mountain lion attacks reported in Montana, Colorado, California, Texas, Arizona and British Columbia. Mountain lions are tan cats that can grow up to 9 feet long, and weigh more than 200 pounds, with 1½-inch claws and 2-inch fangs. They attack by sinking their claws into the shoulder and chest; they have enough strength in their jaws to break a deer's neck.

ATTACKS BY BIG CATS SPREAD FEAR

DENVER — Man and mountain lion are in the throes of a violent struggle for space at the foothills of the Rocky Mountains. After a jogger was killed last month, some say the huge cats have "gone mad."

On January 14, a young man was attacked as he was jogging near his high school in Idaho Springs, west of Denver. Wildlife officials theorize the running may have triggered a "cat-and-mouse" response in the 3-year-old male cougar, which attacked from behind.

In September 1989, a 5-year-old was killed by a mountain lion while riding his tricycle in his front yard in the small wooded town in western Montana. The boy was dragged from the yard and his body was found nearby several hours later.

All kinds of creatures can create great fiction with tension. Don't forget little feathered backyard friends from Hitchcock's *The Birds*, or the shark in Peter Benchley's *Jaws* or the whale in *Moby Dick*.

Sea creatures other than sharks are responsible for deaths. This report of death from stinging by a jellyfish appeared in the *Journal of the American Medical Association*:

SUDDEN DEATH IN A CHILD FOLLOWING JELLYFISH ENVENOMATION

TEXAS—A boy who was 4 years old was swimming in the Gulf of Mexico at Crystal Beach, Texas. At 2 p.m. he began screaming and was carried from the water by his mother; the boy had jellyfish tentacles wrapped around his left arm.

He was transported to a large medical center, but less than 2 hours later, at 3:21 p.m. he was pronounced dead.

Sudden death following stings by jellyfish is well known in Australia where the Pacific box jellyfish, considered the most dangerous marine animal, is indigenous. In the United States, three fatal stings by the Atlantic Portuguese man-of-war have been reported. The little boy mentioned earlier was stung by a sea wasp jellyfish. Acute fatal reactions to jellyfish stings are due to the action of the toxins on the heart and respiratory centers.

While we're on the subject of danger in the outdoors from mountain lions, jellyfish and sharks, let's add another danger—rabies. Rabies is a virus that kills nerve cells in certain portions of the brain. While "rabies" conjures up images of a foaming wild dog, most cases involve bats and skunks. However, rabies has been found in increasing numbers in raccoons in the Southeast, and their numbers have been spreading northward into Pennsylvania and Maryland recently.

Once a person has symptoms after being bitten, the disease is fatal. Death can only be prevented if treatment is started immediately after the bite, and even then it is not always successful. How common is rabies? At least one person a year dies in the United States from rabies. Recently, a man in Texas died from the bite of a rabid bat that he was trying to get out of a friend's house.

What about rabies in fiction? Pete Dexter used rabies quite effectively in his novel *Paris Trout*, when he chronicles the tragic death of a young girl, Rosie Sayers, following the bite of a rabid fox:

In the spring of that year an epidemic of rabies broke out in Ether County, Georgia. The disease was carried principally by foxes and was reported first by farmers, who, in the months of April and May, shot more than seventy of the animals and turned them in to the county health officer in Cotton Point.

Two residents of an outlying area of Cotton Point called Damp Bottoms were reportedly bitten. One of them, an old man known only as Woodrow, was found lying under his house a day later, dead. The other was a fourteen-year-old girl named Rosie Sayers, who was bothered by nightmares.

> Pete Dexter, *Paris Trout* (Penguin)
> —winner of National Book Award

Later Dexter tells us:

She passed the windows wide, averting her eyes, and when she was safely by and looked in front of herself again, she saw the fox. He was dull red and tired and seemed in some way to recognize her.

She knew foxes had turned poisonous from her brothers. Worse than a snake. She stopped again, and he stopped with her. Her brothers said when the poison fox bit you, you were poisonous too.

She never felt the bites. The fox growled—the sound was higher-pitched than a dog, and busier—and then she kicked out with her heels and felt his coat and the bones beneath it.

Later, he simply states, "And Rosie Sayers, fourteen, had died of her wounds."

Food Poisoning

Food poisoning is still a common killer around the world, involving everything from botulism, to mushrooms, to puffer fish in Japan.

POISON MUSHROOMS FATAL TO 16 RUSSIANS
MOSCOW—Sixteen people died and 62 were hospitalized in serious condition after eating poisonous mushrooms near the Russian town of Krasnodar.

The government ordered the people to stop picking and selling mushrooms immediately, until the mushrooms could be studied further.

Here are some statistics from the Centers for Disease Control (CDC) regarding food poisoning:

- In the spring of 1985 more than 200,000 in the Midwest got salmonellosis from contamination with raw milk.
- In 1985 *Listeria* bacteria in soft cheese killed eighty people in California.
- In 1985 botulism from contaminated fish killed two people in New York.
- In 1986 five people died in a Connecticut nursing home from salmonella-infected pureed food.
- In 1986 salmonella in fish made fifty-six people in Washington, D.C., severely ill.
- In 1986 twenty people in New Jersey got salmonellosis from stuffed pasta shells.
- In 1986 nine people became desperately ill from typhoid after eating shrimp salad.

That same CDC report stated that 35,000 Americans were hospitalized in 1985 with salmonellosis, which killed more than 1,000 people and left 120,000 others with chronic crippling diseases like arthritis. Poultry is the main source of salmonellosis. It's hard to cook, and if the meat is red, you may get sick. Salmonella is easy to spread, and if you first handle the raw chicken or turkey and then make a salad without first washing your hands, you could infect the entire dinner party with salmonella.

There are several strains of the bacteria salmonella that can cause food poisoning and enteritis. But one strain, *Salmonella typhi*, is deadly; it is the cause of typhoid fever. With the more common salmonella infection, one usually experiences only a severe gastrointestinal distress with cramps, diarrhea and vomiting. Typhoid fever, however, is a killer, and more than one-third of those infected with *Salmonella typhi* will die. Instead of remaining in the gut like other strains of salmonella, it invades the bloodstream and infects many organs, triggering severe and sometimes fatal inflammation known as typhoid fever.

So, don't forget that you can either kill your characters or make them sick as hell by eating contaminated foods, especially poultry. The food sources mentioned will help you plot their demise. The most common food poisonings by bacteria include botulism, salmonella, typhoid fever and staphylococcus (common in potato salads with mayonnaise, egg dishes and chicken salads).

Most of the infections listed are the result of ingesting the bacteria, which then grow in the intestines of the victim and secrete toxins that produce the disease. Botulism is different; the bacteria grows in canned or sealed foods and excrete the toxin into the food. The victim dies soon after eating the toxic food (not as a result of the bacteria growing in the intestines).

The Clostridium bacteria that cause botulism grow in improperly canned foods. If food is not pressure-cooked or boiled long enough, then the bacterial spores are not killed. Home-canned vegetables (especially tomatoes, beans and meats) are the most common foods involved. However, the toxin is very heat sensitive and can be broken down and made harmless by boiling or heating the food to more than 100° Celsius for a minute or two.

The botulism toxin blocks the neuromuscular junction and causes paralysis. After eating the toxic food, the victim becomes weak, paralysis sets in rapidly and the person dies from respiratory paralysis. There is a trivalent antitoxin available from the CDC; respiratory support needs to be given during the treatment.

An excellent review of all types of poisonings can be found in *Deadly Doses* (Writer's Digest Books) by Stevens and Klarner, and I highly recommend it as a reference book.

Specific Accidents

A recent article in the *Journal of the American Medical Association* (JAMA) reported that over one thousand teenagers have been killed by Coke machines. It sounds absurd, but it's true. Teenage boys, mad about losing their quarters to stubborn machines, wrestle with them to get their change back; the heavy machines tumble back and crush their victims. As mentioned earlier, in one year, more than twelve thousand infants and children were injured by falling out of grocery carts! More than 180 infants have drowned by falling into household cleaning buckets. One hundred sixty adults were killed by garage door openers! And forty-seven children crushed when the door closed on them.

Deadly Winter

According to the Centers for Disease Control, more than twenty thousand people die in the United States each year because of winter. The causes of death include heart attacks, falling on ice, car wrecks from bad road conditions, and faulty heaters causing fires or carbon monoxide poisoning.

In January 1992, the largest snow storm in a decade hit Detroit, dumping more than a foot of snow. At least twenty-two people died the following day. Many died shoveling snow or pushing cars out of drifts. They were folks in relatively good health, some exercised regularly, and some were long-distance runners. Why did they die? Possible reasons are:

- classic heart attack
- cold-air induced spasm of coronary vessels with fatal arrhythmias (usually accounting for deaths in healthy individuals).

In Milwaukee, an average of ten to twelve people die after each big snowfall. These deaths are as predictable as the snow itself; cold air from the north bringing snow, clogged roads and death.

Falling

There are two ways you can **fall**: a vertical "controlled" fall, with the person landing upright and feet-first; and an "uncontrolled" fall, with some other part of the body hitting first, such as landing on your back, head, stomach, etc.

The vertical controlled fall is survivable up to more than 100 feet, but an uncontrolled fall can be fatal at very short distances, such as falling from a stepladder. With a vertical fall, the initial energy is transmitted through the feet and legs, sparing vital organs. But an uncontrolled fall can cause massive head injury, torn liver and spleen, torn lungs, or shearing of the heart or the aorta with fatal, massive blood loss.

The important thing to remember is that you can "kill" one of your characters by having them fall short distances, or survive falls from great heights if your plot calls for it.

TRAPEZE ARTIST DIES IN FALL WITHOUT NET
MARQUETTE—A young circus trapeze artist performing without a net died when she fell 28 feet to the ground.

She was spinning on a rope when she fell, suffering internal injuries.

This unfortunate accident was most likely an "uncontrolled" fall because a height of 28 feet proved fatal.

Controlled fall: A controlled fall is when someone lands directly on their feet. The legs, pelvis and back all act in concert to absorb the energy of the fall, and while the person may sustain significant injuries to internal organs as well as fractures, survival from a very high fall up to 100 feet or more is possible.

Uncontrolled fall: An uncontrolled fall is when one lands on a part of their body other than the feet, such as back, stomach, head, etc. An uncontrolled fall such as this can be fatal from very short distances in the range of 15 to 20 feet.

The Cafe Coronary

Ever hear of it? The correct term is asphyxiation by food, or choking to death from food lodged in the throat.

This accident usually happens in a restaurant after the victim has had one or two drinks, then takes a bite of steak while talking or laughing. This is also common in backyard barbecues, with people drinking beer while trying to down steaks overdone on the grill.

It appears as if the victim is having a heart attack; thus the term **cafe coronary**. Food lodges firmly in the throat, preventing both breathing and talking, so the victim cannot even tell someone that he is in fact choking. He grabs his throat in a panic, and fear is painted on his face as he turns blue while he slowly and agonizingly chokes to death in front of everyone, unable to talk, unable to breathe.

In 1973 before the **Heimlich maneuver** became popular, there were over two thousand five hundred such fatalities that year. Choking ranked sixth in the United States among the causes of accidental death—well ahead of aircraft accidents, firearms, lightning and death from snakebites.

How does the Heimlich maneuver work? Even when the airway is completely closed off, there is a residual volume of air trapped in the spongy lung tissue that can be used to force the impacted food out of the throat and save the person's life.

It seems that humans are the only species cursed with this problem. Animals that are carnivorous usually rip large pieces of flesh from the carcass of their kill and gulp it down in huge chunks. They have to eat fast before the food is stolen by another predator. Birds can swallow a whole fish. Yet none of these ever chokes on food, even large pieces.

Why? Because they can't talk.

Homo sapiens evolved with the most complex voice pattern of any animal on earth, allowing them to develop sophisticated speech. But this happened at a cost; in order to produce the complex voice pattern, it was necessary for the vocal cords to be very close together, and the airway at this location to be very narrow. With the evolution of voice came a life-threatening potential for choking, either from food stuck in the throat or from the complications of infections, such as diphtheria or epiglottitis.

A Fatal Blow

A recent case in New York created an outpouring of sympathy from the public when the unusual death of a twelve-year-old boy was published. He was playing softball in the park with friends; the ball hit him squarely in the chest, and he fell over dead.

This is a well-known phenomenon: A sudden, forceful blow or impact to the chest may cause instantaneous cardiac arrest without any visible damage to either the chest wall or the heart. The blow causes a jolt to the electrical circuit of the nerves within the heart that control its rhythmic contraction, and the heart becomes still. And strangely, the impact doesn't have to be severe; often a minor, direct blow to the center of the chest is enough to cause instant death.

This unusual cause of death was recounted in two novels by well-known authors. In the first scene, the coroner's assistant is explaining this unusual cause of death to the detective:

> "It's quite possible this is a case of what we call death from inhibition. Instantaneous physiological death."
>
> "Meaning what?"
>
> He shrugged. "The person just dies."
>
> "For no reason at all?"
>
> "Well, not exactly. There's usually minor trauma involving the heart or nerves. But the trauma isn't sufficient to cause death. I had one case where a ten-year-old kid got hit in the chest with a baseball—not very hard—and fell down dead in the school yard. Nobody within twenty meters of him. Another case, a woman had a minor car accident, banged into the steering wheel with her chest, not very hard, and while she was opening the car door to get out, she dropped dead."
>
> Michael Crichton, *Rising Sun* (Knopf)

In this scene, the protagonist, who is a medical examiner for New York City, has been assigned the case and is struggling with her feelings about a boy's death:

> Her thoughts turned to the case that had bothered her the most over the weekend; the twelve-year-old boy hit in the chest with a softball.
>
> ... Up until the accident, the softball victim had been a healthy child, brimming with health and vitality. Without any

positive finding on the autopsy, she would need personal accounts to substantiate her diagnosis of commotio cordis, or death from a blow to the chest.

Robin Cook, *Blindsight* (Putnam)

A Breath of Death

Teenagers looking for a new high inhale the fumes from common household products such as glue, typewriter correction fluid, gasoline, solvents, nail polish remover, cooking spray, propane and aerosol sprays.

All of these give a sense of euphoria, followed by depression. The temporary neurological problems include paralysis, weakness, dizziness, lack of coordination and muscle spasm. After a short initial high, the person becomes dizzy and uncoordinated. In some, there is cardiac arrest and death, depending on the amount inhaled.

Life Is a Risky Affair

According to the *New England Journal of Medicine*, left-handed people live nine years less than right-handed people. The average right-hander dies at age seventy-five, the average southpaw dies at sixty-six. For some reason lefties have a higher accident rate: Eight percent of lefties died from accident-related injuries versus 1.5 percent for right-handers. The reason postulated for this is that motorized vehicles, power tools and safety levers are all designed for right-handed use. The reflex of lefties is therefore reduced.

Every fifty minutes someone dies from a work-related accident; every twenty-three minutes, from an accident in the home; every eleven minutes, in an auto wreck.

The riskiest sport is hang-gliding, with a death rate of 114 per 100,000. Next is parachuting, followed by rock climbing.

More than ten thousand workers die each year on the job. That's about thirty every day. What do you think is the most dangerous occupation—a cop? Fireman? Or perhaps a miner? Not even close. The most dangerous occupation is farming. Agriculture tops the list of dangerous occupational fields, followed by construction, then mining.

There is danger down on the farm. More than one thousand five hundred died in a recent year in farm accidents, and harvest time is the bloodiest season. Tractor rollovers are the number-one killer. Each year more than four thousand children and adolescents are injured by farm accidents and more than 190 are killed.

Causes of Death on the Farm

- Crushed under tractor rollovers
- Electrocuted from contact with power lines
- Caught in corn pickers
- Buried and suffocated in corn bins
- Crushed by cattle
- Suffocated in hay
- Strangled by clothing caught in power take-off
- Suffocated by fumes or gases in silo

And, several times a day, everyone goes to a potentially hazardous place — the bathroom! The place where people bathe, smoke, read and conduct business is where 25 percent of all household accidents occur. Three percent of all fatal home accidents, more than 200,000 nonfatal injuries and numerous drownings occur in the bathroom.

Hair dryers near the tub or shower, razors, chemical cleaners, poisons, medicines and slippery floors can all be deadly. More than 350 people drown in the tub each year.

Life in general is a crapshoot. Women wearing super-absorbent tampons are at risk of dying from Toxic Shock Syndrome. Killer bees are now reported in Texas and have been responsible for dozens of deaths in South and Central America. JAMA reported an illness called the "Sick Santa Syndrome" because young children are exposed to communicable illnesses such as influenza and tuberculosis that many of the temporarily employed Santas carry. When sitting on Santa's knee to ask for a new Barbie can be fatal, you know life is a risky affair.

What Are Your Chances?

Your chances of dying by a terrorist's hand if you travel overseas:	1 in 650,000
Your chances of dying from skiing:	1 in 500,000
Your chances of dying from rock climbing:	1 in 5,000
Your chances of dying from parachuting:	1 in 4,000

You'll Increase Your Chances of Dying by One in a Million if You

■ Travel 10 miles by bicycle
■ Spend one hour in a coal mine
■ Smoke 1.4 cigarettes
■ Live with a smoker for two months

Electrocution

Each year in the United States there are more than five hundred deaths from lightning (high-energy direct current) and more than one thousand deaths from household current (low-energy alternating current).

While the physics of electricity can be confusing, we can simplify it somewhat: First, there are two types of electrical current: AC (alternating current) and DC (direct current).

Direct Current (DC)

Direct current means that the voltage and direction of the current stays constant. DC is produced by batteries and by lightning. (See the section on lightning later in this chapter.)

Direct current causes more injury to the body (tissue damage and burns) than does alternating current of the same voltage.

Alternating Current (AC)

Even though a direct current causes more actual tissue damage from heat and burning, an electrical shock from AC is considered to be *more deadly* because it kills by instantaneous ventricular fibrillation of the heart. The heart muscle "quivers" but does not have effective pumping action; death will follow quickly if the circulation is not restored immediately by means of either mechanical CPR or electrical defibrillator.

AC current is divided into high and low voltages:

• Low voltage is less than 1,000 volts
• High voltage is more than 1,000 volts

Even a low-voltage 110 AC shock from a household outlet can be fatal because it alters the electrical pattern of the heart, resulting in ventricular fibrillation. The repetitive 60 cycles per second current alters the heart's electrical impulses, and the heart goes into ventricular fibrillation, followed by cardiac arrest and death. Dropping or throwing an electrical appliance into the bathtub can produce a fatal cardiac arrhythmia, yet leave little or no external visible sign of injury.

How Serious Is the Injury?

All electrical injuries, whether produced by household current or lightning, cause a characteristic wound pattern on the skin at the entrance site. This consists of a central pale area with a peripheral zone that is bright red where blood has been pushed by the heat generated in the electrical charge.

Several factors determine the seriousness of accidental electrocution. These include amperage, type of current (AC vs. DC), duration of the contact, path of the current, voltage and resistance.

Amperage: This is the amount of current flowing and is a major factor in the extent of injury. Greater flow (more amperage) will cause more heat and therefore more tissue damage. As a rule, the extent of injury is proportional to amperage. One amp may cause ventricular fibrillation of the heart, 2 amps will cause burns, and more than 10 amps will cause the heart to stop beating (asystole).

Types of current: Alternating current (household electricity) is more dangerous than direct current (example, from a battery) because the alternating cycle can cause the heart to stop beating. Also, AC current can cause the muscles to contract, freezing the victim to the source. DC direct current causes injury by burning.

Duration of contact: The longer the person is in contact with the electrical source, the greater is the degree of heat and therefore tissue damage.

Path of current: Electricity must have a path through the body, with an entry and an exit. Both places will show evidence of burn. But the path inside the body between these two places is very important. If the flow is from leg-to-leg, it is not as important as from the head-to-leg, where the brain, heart and other organs are injured.

When an electric chair is used, a metal cap is placed on the prisoner's head and a metal plate strapped to the foot before electrocution, because the path of the current is directed through the brain, through all vital organs, and finally, out the leg.

Voltage: A current of 1,000 volts or more is considered high voltage. High-voltage injury from lightning or high-tension power lines will cause extensive injury with charred areas of skin where entry and exit occurred, and asystole (absence of contractions) of the heart. The muscles and deep tissues become swollen and rock-hard, evidence of extensive injury and burn.

The usual household current of 110 volts AC may merely cause a painful shock that stuns the victim. But if the current passes from the hand through the foot to the ground, passing through the heart, fatal ventricular fibrillation may result.

Household current of 110 volts can be deadly and presents particular danger to children. A child who bites through an electrical cord may have facial injury and disfigurement. There may be massive bleeding from the mouth because the arteries in the mouth and gum are burned and bleed excessively. The focal tissue necrosis where the child bites into the cord causes erosion of labial (lip) arteries, resulting in tremendous bleeding from the mouth of the child.

Activities of Children Leading to Electrical Injury	
Oral contact with cord	28%
Foreign object placed in wall socket	28%
Faulty wall socket or plug	17%
Faulty cord	15%
Misuse of cord or socket	12%

In the adult, the greatest risk from low-voltage shock is a change in heart rhythm. With either fibrillation (heart quivering but not beating) or asystole (heart stopped) the result may be fatal.

The injury from high voltage is due to the production of heat with electrothermal burning and charring of tissues, whereas low voltage stops the heart activity. Death in the bathtub from a hair dryer or radio is by the same mechanism: The 110-volt AC current causes death from ventricular fibrillation of the heart. In this case, there may be no evidence of damage, or only a small area of burn on the skin where the current passed through.

Was it murder, accident or suicide? That may be difficult to ascertain. Electrocution is a very unusual method for suicide, and even if it were a suicide, in most instances the person would be fully clothed, not nude. It is almost impossible to determine the intent of death, whether accident or murder. Suffice it to say that a fair number of people die each year from accidental electrocution.

Lightning

"I heard a boom. It was the loudest sound I ever heard in my life. He fell backwards. He made no sound at all." The seventeen-year-old boy had just witnessed the death of his friend on a baseball field.

Lightning is a natural phenomenon that produces millions of volts and very high amperes. A single bolt may carry over 100 million volts of direct current and reach 50,000° Fahrenheit. The main bolt causes massive tissue damage, burning and charring, sometimes causing a limb to swell, burn and split open like a grilled hot dog. Superheated air from lightning can turn the sweat on a person's body to steam, and blast their clothes off (literally knocking their socks off). It can also lift the person off the ground or throw them in the air. Millions of volts in a single strike can cook nerves, damage the brain, form cataracts, rupture eardrums, break bones and sizzle skin — all in under a second.

When a person is struck by lightning and the current passes through the brain, there is an immediate loss of consciousness, breathing stops, and the heart spasms into a tight contraction. After a short period of time, the heart muscle will relax and may resume normal spontaneous beating. If the damage to the brain is minimal, recovery may be possible. But if there is considerable burn damage of the brain tissues, death is certain.

Most people struck by lightning are hit by a stray current from the main bolt, not by the main bolt itself. These people with stray hits are merely stunned and have stiff, sore muscles and possibly small burns where the current exited. For every person killed by lightning, there are at least three who are struck by nonlethal charges.

The following is a true account of a young woman struck by lightning, published in *Reader's Digest*. This probably describes a stray hit rather than one by the main bolt:

The next instant, the world exploded around her in bright, paralyzing light.

The pulsing channel of lightning entered Mary's body with an ear-splitting crack, lifting her off the ground. Her muscles contracted violently, and electricity sent her blood vessels into spasms, cutting off blood flow to her extremities. Her hair stood on end.

As the charge surged down her legs, searing nerves and muscle tissue, the acrid smell of burning flesh filled Mary's nostrils. She stood riveted in the pure white heat.

Finally, the paralyzing assault stopped, and Mary fell to the ground.

Reported by Deborah Morris in *Reader's Digest*,
April 1991

Injury Related to Electrical Currents

Direct Current:
- Source: batteries, lightning
- Injuries: thermal injury with tissue burning and charring

High-voltage Alternating Current:
- Source: high-tension wires, transformers
- Injuries: extensive deep tissue injury and burns, lethal asystole of the heart

Low-voltage Alternating Current:
- Source: standard household current, outlets
- Injuries: massive bleeding from the mouth in children who bite through cords; fatal ventricular fibrillation or asystole of the heart

Death Among Children

Injuries are the leading cause of death among children under the age of nineteen.

Motor Vehicle Crashes

According to the Centers for Disease Control, auto accidents accounted for half of the 22,411 fatal childhood injuries in the United States in 1990. Seventy percent were occupants of a car, while 17 percent were pedestrians.

Homicide

Homicide accounted for 13 percent of fatal injuries among children. Two-thirds of these were among fifteen- to nineteen-year-olds.

Suicide

Suicide was the third leading cause of childhood fatal injuries. Eighty percent of these were in the ten- to nineteen-year-old group. Firearms were used in 60 percent of the deaths.

Drowning

Drowning, the fourth leading cause of childhood fatal injuries, was most common among those under the age of four, and among males fifteen to nineteen. In the older group, alcohol was a common factor in many of the drownings.

Fires and Burns

Fires and burns were the fifth leading cause of childhood fatal injury: Eighty percent from house fires; 9 percent from electrical burns; and 2 percent from scalding.

Child Abuse

A final sad word about death among children. Child abuse is a major cause of childhood injuries. It is estimated that 1.6 million children in the United States suffer from abuse or neglect, which includes: violent attacks, beating, rape, incest, malnourishment or psychological brutality.

Accident Prevention Would Help

Each year nearly sixteen million emergency room visits are due to childhood injury, with more than 30,000 resulting in permanent disability and 22,411 deaths. Many accidents could be avoided by the use of seatbelts, smoke detectors and fire alarms, enclosures around swimming pools, inaccessibility of firearms, and better intervention and education for parents at high risk of becoming child abusers.

Emergency Treatment and Transportation

"Can you hear me?" shouts a flight surgeon, flashing a light in each eye. "Can you hear me?"

No response. One pupil is abnormally dilated; a chalky white fragment of femoral bone sticks straight out from a huge gash in the boy's leg.

The twisted motorcycle is off to the side of the road, bleeding gasoline and oil onto the pavement. An eighteen-wheeler, unscathed except for a bent grill, is parked 500 yards down the road. An I.V. is started, a splint put over the leg, then the boy is quickly loaded onto the waiting helicopter as the medical team races against death.

In this scene, the motorcycle rider received prompt treatment and was transported expediently to a proper medical facility with a shock-trauma unit. But this service is not always available, and many people who might have been saved will die because of delayed treatment.

The Emergency Medical Services System Act

In November 1973, the Emergency Medical Services System Act (EMSS) (Public Law 93-154) was signed into law by President Nixon. This established regional emergency services throughout the country. The growing **EMS** network has seen a growth in the transporting and treatment of injured victims to regional emergency facilities. Helicopters have become commonplace in most areas of the country for transporting critically injured people.

Accidents today are the leading killer of Americans under the age of forty-four. And for many, the line between life and death is determined not by the seriousness of the accident, but by the location of the accident. The well-organized EMS teams piece together bodies shattered by car crashes, gunshot wounds, fires and near-drownings until the victims can be treated at an emergency facility.

The problem is that most areas in the U.S. do not have such a system, and the unlucky ones become double victims — of both their injuries and of geography. Each year seventy million Americans are hurt in accidents; approximately 140,000 die. If all accident victims received state-of-the-art care, then one in five deaths could be prevented, saving twenty thousand lives a year. But trauma is overlooked as a major killer, and funds are shifted to other areas of health care.

The Golden Hour

The first sixty minutes after injury are called the "golden hour" because more than 70 percent of all deaths occur within that time.

If treatment is started within that first hour, the victim has a much greater chance of survival. The causes of death from trauma are:

- Head injury (50 percent)
- Hemorrhage and massive blood loss (35 percent)
- Airway compromise or lung damage (15 percent)

When an accident victim is first seen, the basic priorities are the same as in the ER: Check if the patient is breathing; measure the pulse; look for any gross external bleeding. Note that spinal injury is considered only after these others have been assessed.

A Final Word

The most important thing to take away from this chapter is simply this: You don't have to *murder* your characters to have them die in the story. Having grandpa die falling from a ladder while picking apples can create more empathy than shooting the old man in the head during a robbery. Accidents, from the mundane to the bizarre, provide a powerful, emotional writing device, both to enrich the plot and provide new opportunities for story development and change.

SUDDEN DEATH

There may be a time when your plot calls for a character to die suddenly. But don't forget that characters must act out of *their* needs, not the writer's. The need for a character's death must come from the plot.

Don't kill the hero's father suddenly just because you don't know what to do with him, he is getting in the way, or you think it may be dramatic. If this happens, it signals a problem in the plot and you need to backtrack to where the plot derails and *fix it*.

But, if your plot is solid and the story calls for a character to die suddenly, this chapter will help you accomplish it by using something more than just the unimaginative "hit by a car" ploy.

The Use of Sudden Death in Literature

Sudden death from natural causes is rarely used in literature; in modern fiction, most characters meet their untimely demise from an accident or homicide.

Sudden death from natural causes is not common in fiction because it doesn't serve the needs of the plot as well as chronic illness or murder. By using chronic illness and disease with the inevitable slow death, the writer can create empathy for the dying character. There is time for characters to reflect on death (their own or someone else's) and there is time for *change*.

A sudden death from murder has dramatic tension because a crime has been committed, and the motives of the murderer as well as his eventual capture and punishment all become elements of the plot.

Sudden deaths from accidents are easy for us to relate to because we all have accidents, see them constantly on TV, read about them in the papers and see them happen on the streets. As the preceding chapter pointed out, accidental death is frequently used in fiction.

A sudden death from natural causes requires special circumstances and must be used carefully because many of the elements needed for enhancing the plot are missing (motive, crime and punishment, theme of death). However, a sudden death from natural causes can still be an effective tool.

Here is a scene from the end of *Doctor Zhivago*. Zhivago is certain that he has spotted the woman he once "loved and lost" years ago, so he fights his way off the trolley and through the crowds toward her:

> Her course was parallel to that of the trolley. Yurii Zhivago had already lost sight of her several times. The doctor felt an attack of nausea coming on. Surmounting his weakness, he got up and jerked the window straps, trying to open the window.
>
> He continued his attempts to open the window and gave three sharp tugs. Suddenly he felt a sharp pain, greater than any he had ever experienced before; he realized that something had broken in him, he had done something irreparable, fatal, that this was the end.
>
> By a superhuman effort of the will, Yurii Zhivago pushed through the crowd; people blocked his way and snapped at him. Ignoring the resentful cries, he broke through the crowd, got down from the trolley into the street, took a step, another, a third, collapsed on the stone paving and did not get up again.

Several people surrounded him and soon found that he was not breathing and that his heart had stopped.

The lady in lilac came up too, stood a moment, looked at the body, and went on. She had come to Moscow for her exit visa. So she walked on, overtaking the trolley for the tenth time and quite unaware that she had overtaken Zhivago and survived him.

Boris Pasternak, *Doctor Zhivago*

That is a powerful scene, made more tragic by his sudden death from a heart attack, almost as if the fates prevented him from reaching his old love one final time.

What Constitutes a Sudden Death

Sudden death is an unexpected, nontraumatic, non-self-inflicted fatality that occurs within six hours of the terminal event. Sudden death is the leading mode of death in the industrialized world.

In the United States, more than 500,000 sudden deaths occur annually. More than half of these succumb to instantaneous death, which occurs within seconds in people who were engaged in normal activity immediately prior to their collapse.

Most of these instantaneous deaths are the result of **ventricular tachycardia** (VT) and ventricular fibrillation (VF), arrhythmias of the heart.

Ventricular Tachycardia (Called "V-tach" or "VT"): A very rapid heart rate, which by itself is usually nonfatal, but may go directly into fatal ventricular fibrillation.

Ventricular Fibrillation (Called "V-fib" or "VF"): This is a "twitching" of the ventricular muscle of the heart; the electrical impulses are so rapid and erratic that normal coordinated contractions cannot occur.

Sudden death associated with either ventricular tachycardia or fibrillation is almost always associated with **arteriosclerotic** coronary artery disease.

This chapter deals only with sudden death from natural causes (all deaths not from murder, suicide or accident). (See chapter nine on accidental deaths.) Sudden deaths in adults from natural causes happen in real life more frequently than commonly supposed. More than 60 percent of all cases investigated by the coroner's office are found to be from natural causes.

Sudden, unexpected deaths usually become a coroner's case and a medical-legal autopsy is required to establish the cause of death (the disease or injury that initiated events resulting in death) and the manner of death (natural, suicide, homicide or accident).

A violent death (accident, suicide, homicide) may sometimes be difficult to recognize and may be erroneously labeled natural causes. For instance, a fatal electrical shock can occur with only a very tiny (and easily overlooked) electrical burn. If the death is caused by 110-volt alternating current entering and exiting the body through wide, moist surfaces, there will be no visible skin injury, despite the fact that the electrical shock caused ventricular fibrillation (heart muscle quivers without pumping) and death. This is the scenario of a hair dryer or radio falling into a bathtub and causing fatal shock. Many deaths from poison also give no external clues. Blunt head trauma can be fatal with no visible external signs; this can also happen with trauma to the chest or abdomen.

One of the most common causes of sudden death results from degenerative changes of the body (such as rupture of aneurysm, heart attack, massive fatal stroke), changes that are clinically silent and without symptoms until the sudden death. This is obviously most frequent in the older population; and men by far outnumber women as victims of sudden death due to a slow progressive degeneration of the body.

While not always necessary, it may be appropriate for you to "plant" the cause of death early in the story. Showing a person having problems with dizziness, then later falling down the stairs seems quite appropriate to the reader. Or a person with high blood pressure may have a stroke. A chain smoker who is under constant pressure may have a fatal heart attack. A person with diabetes may have a diabetic coma (as in the movie *Steel Magnolias*).

Common Causes of Sudden Death

Here is a list of causes of sudden death (usually instantaneous death, but it may occur within a period of six hours) that you might consider for use in your story:

Specific Causes of Sudden Death

- Heart attack
- Stroke
- Seizure and drowning
- Ruptured aorta
- Pulmonary embolus
- Fainting while driving, fatal crash
- Diabetic coma
- Ruptured stomach ulcer
- Asthma attack
- Complictions of labor and delivery
- Death from physiological shock (hemorrhaging)
- Death from psychological shock (scared to death)

Natural Causes of Sudden Death	Percent
Diseases of heart, aorta, blood vessels	42
Diseases of respiratory tract	23
Disease of brain and meninges	9
Disease of urogenital and digestive tract (kidneys, intestines)	13
Miscellaneous	13

Cardiovascular System

The most frequent causes of adult sudden death are related to the cardiovascular system: stroke, heart attack, blood clot (embolus) of the pulmonary artery, or ruptured aorta with massive fatal hemorrhage.

Worked to death: In downtown Tokyo, a man falls forward on his face and hits the sidewalk hard, as if someone smashed him with a baseball bat. He is a thin, medium-sized man; a filter-tipped Mild Seven cigarette lies beside him, smoldering where it fell.

A crowd gathers, murmuring. Someone turns him over, and

the bone-colored skin and vacant eyes tell the story that he is already dead.

"**Karoshi**," someone whispers. "**Karoshi**."

A paramedic arrives and the fallen man is lifted by stretcher into the ambulance and carted off to the morgue. The people who saw him fall were long gone; it was growing dark, and for most of them, there was still work to do.

This sobering account was detailed by Pete Hamill in *Esquire*. The word karoshi means "sudden death because of overwork." The average victim is a male in his forties or fifties. The cause of death is usually a sudden fatal heart attack or cerebral hemorrhage brought on by stress or too many hours on the job.

Anxiety can kill, and in Tokyo, there is a lot of anxiety and constant pressure to succeed; the worry about losing "face" or one's honor is always present.

Heart attack: Of the 500,000 cases of sudden death each year in the United States, more than 300,000 are due to cardiac arrest following heart attacks.

The medical term for heart attack is myocardial infarction, or "MI." "Myocardial" refers to the muscular tissue of the heart, and "infarction" means death and necrosis (breakdown and lysis) of tissue due to obstruction of the vascular supply to the area. That is to say, a heart attack or "MI" is death to a portion of the heart muscle because it suddenly has its blood shut off either by clot or by vessels occluded by disease.

The symptoms of an acute MI are commonly known, and include sudden severe chest pain, pain in the left arm that radiates into the neck, and nausea, or "upset stomach." The heart may suddenly stop beating or go into ventricular fibrillation—in which case the person suddenly falls over dead. This is what happened to Zhivago, first experiencing nausea and chest pain, then collapsing on the sidewalk with sudden death. Or, the death of the heart muscle may be slower, and the person may survive until medical help arrives.

Scared to death: The common terms "scared to death" and "frightened to death" may be reality. The sudden massive release of epinephrine following extreme terror or fear can cause ventricular fibrillation of the heart, leading to death. (See chapter twelve on voodoo, emotional stress and sudden death.)

Stroke: Stroke is the brain's equivalent to a heart attack. A sudden blockage of blood supply to a portion of the brain results in death to the nerve cells. A stroke is also called a "cerebral vascular accident" or "CVA."

The symptoms of a stroke depend on which part of the brain is affected. A person may die suddenly on the spot; have severe headache; become comatose and die; or have a nonfatal stroke with damage to the brain causing paralysis to one side of the body, loss of speech, loss of vision (cortical blindness), loss of ability to understand, or loss of cognition and awareness of self (frontal lobe infarction).

As you will see in chapter eleven on chronic illness, a stroke can either cause sudden death or a slow, lingering death. So, when one of your characters suffers a stroke, you can burden him or her with virtually any kind of disability needed for the plot and still be medically correct. Some people lose short-term memory; others long-term memory. Some are confined to wheelchairs and become almost infantile or are totally unaware of their surroundings; others recover with minimal deficits.

Here is an example of how sudden death might be used as an important plot point: A young pregnant woman notes with dismay that her water has broken, she goes into labor immediately and delivers a baby boy two weeks early. The baby has severe difficulty breathing, and before they can get him to the hospital forty minutes away, the baby is dead. The wife is now furious with her husband because it was he who insisted that they live on a ranch, thirty miles from the nearest town; she blames the baby's death on him.

The plot possibilities following the infant's death are numerous: It may affect a marriage; cause guilt in the doctor who couldn't save the infant; cause drastic inner conflict in either the mother or father, depending on the circumstances.

This is just one example to show how a sudden death throws characters into conflict, allowing any number of plot lines to develop from it.

Chronic Illness and Disease

There may be times when your plot calls for a character to either live with a debilitating disease or to slowly waste away from a fatal illness. When used properly, chronic illness with a slow death can be a forceful tool in fiction. This allows time in the story for the author to develop a character's reaction to his own or someone else's death. Death itself may become the antagonist against which the characters must struggle. Or the disease may provide for a change in direction of the plot and bring about the denouement.

The Use of Chronic Illness in Literature

Chronic illnesses have been widely used in literature because they provide rich opportunities to develop the theme of death. Chronic illnesses that authors have used include leprosy, diabetes, syphilis, viral myocarditis, **consumption (tuberculosis)**, leukemia, cancers of all types and abdominal tumors (especially in women). Although a new mother's death following childbirth is not in reality a chronic illness, the dying process is not always immediate and thus the writer has time to develop a framework for her death: She may have time to suffer and to talk to her family. With these criteria in mind, death from childbirth can be considered in the general context of chronic illness since it provides similar elements for the writer to consider.

Here are some examples to illustrate how common this theme is in fiction and to show how the list of diseases is far more extensive and exotic than you may have thought.

In William Kennedy's Pulitzer Prize-winning *Ironweed*, Helen dies of a tumorous abdomen.

> And then Helen, still wearing that black rag of a coat rather than expose the even more tattered blouse and skirt that she wore beneath it, standing on her spindle legs with her tumorous belly butting the metal stand of the microphone and giving her the look of a woman five months pregnant, casting boldly before the audience this image of womanly disaster. . . .
>
> William Kennedy, *Ironweed* (Penguin)

Pearl S. Buck uses the same disease in *The Good Earth* when O-lan dies from an enlarged tumorous abdomen. The doctor examining O-lan tells her husband:

> "The spleen is enlarged and the liver diseased. There is a rock as large as a man's head in the womb; the stomach is disintegrated. The heart barely moves and there are worms in it."

Later, Buck describes O-lan's slow, painful death:

> But there was no sudden dying of life in O-lan's body. She was scarcely past the middle of her span of years, and her life would not easily pass from her body, so that she lay dying on her bed for many months.

Many authors use death from childbirth or miscarriage very effectively to kill a character and to evoke strong feelings of empathy in the reader. Margaret Mitchell used this ploy effectively in *Gone With the Wind* when she had Melanie die from a miscarriage, thus allowing Scarlett to pursue Melanie's husband, Ashley, whom she had coveted from the beginning of the book.

In Thornton Wilder's Pulitzer Prize-winning play *Our Town*, the main character, Emily, dies in childbirth; Wilder uses her death to define the gulf between the living and the dead.

Cancers of all types have been important in fiction for many years. There are probably several reasons for this. First, the word *cancer* conjures up a cold fear, a desperation, and helplessness. John Wayne's character suffered cancer in *The Shootist* and Bette Davis's character had a brain tumor in *Dark Victory*. In *Terms of Endearment*, by Larry McMurtry, and *The Devil's Advocate*, by Morris West, cancer is the core of the plot that motivates and brings about changes in the main character.

In Tennessee Williams's Pulitzer Prize-winning play, *Cat on a Hot Tin Roof*, the plot revolves around the family gathering to celebrate Big Daddy's birthday, but the importance of it is that since he is dying of cancer, it will be his last.

Doctor:	But now, you see, Big Mama, they cut a piece off this growth, a specimen of the tissue and—
Big Mama:	You told Big Daddy—
Doctor:	Yes, we told Big Daddy. But we had this bit of tissue run through the laboratory and I'm sorry to say the test was positive. It's—well—malignant . . .
Big Mama:	Cancer?! Why didn't they cut it out of him? Hanh?
Doctor:	Involved too much, Big Mama, too many organs affected.
Mae:	Big Mama, the liver's affected and so's the kidneys, both! It's gone way past what they call a—
Gooper:	A surgical risk.

Leukemia is a cancer that affects the blood cells. While great strides have been made and hundreds of people are treated successfully, it remains a dreadful disease with a high mortality rate.

Leukemia has been a fertile subject in both movies and fiction because of the ultimate horror of the disease; it is not disfiguring, the person is awake and alert, but suffering. While leukemia is a terrible disease, it serves the writer well. It is the ultimate "ticking clock" as the disease runs its course to its almost always fatal end. Examples of leukemia in fiction include *Love Story*, by Eric Segal, and *Dying Young*, by Marti Leimbach.

Unusual diseases are sometimes used very effectively. *Of Hu-*

man Bondage deals with a young woman with syphilis. In *Beaches*, Barbara Hershey's character is dying a slow death from viral myocarditis, a viral inflammation of the heart that usually follows a bout of flu and causes a slow, progressive weakening and eventual failure of the heart.

Correlating the Time Period for Your Story

The diseases you inflict on your characters should reflect the era in which your story takes place. If you are writing a Civil War story similar to *Gone With the Wind*, the diseases suffered in the nineteenth century are different from those found in New York City in the 1990s. Typhus, tuberculosis, gangrene, diphtheria, smallpox and childbirth fever were common then; today, hepatitis, AIDS, heart attacks and syphilis are more prevalent and reflect changes in society.

At the turn of the century (before the invention of antibiotics) the leading causes of death were mostly the acute infectious diseases such as influenza, gastritis, diphtheria, pertussis (whooping cough) and pneumonia. As the elderly became progressively debilitated from age, they often developed pneumonia and died quietly in their sleep. Because pneumonia produced a gentle death, it was referred to as the "old man's friend."

Today the leading causes of death are chronic degenerative diseases such as cancer, heart disease and stroke. Unlike pneumonia, these often result in extended suffering and pain before death.

Plagues and Scourges

Tuberculosis

Death from "consumption" (an obsolete term for tuberculosis) has been popular in literature. *Camille*, a play written by Alexandre Dumas, deals with this theme. This popular story was made into both a movie starring Greta Garbo and an opera, *La Traviata*, by Verdi. In another famous opera, *La Bohème*, by Puccini, another young woman, Mimi, dies of tuberculosis.

But is tuberculosis an out-of-date disease that has no place in modern fiction? Not by a long shot. In 1990, there were more than twenty-three thousand cases of tuberculosis in the United States, and TB accounts for more than three million deaths annually around the globe.

Here is an article that appeared recently in the newspaper:

TUBERCULOSIS MAKING A DEADLY COMEBACK IN USA

Tuberculosis, once the nation's leading killer, is reaching epidemic levels in major cities throughout America. Poverty, an increasing homeless population, drug addicts and AIDS all fuel the resurgence of the disease.

It is feared that tuberculosis will devastate low-income neighborhoods unless something is done soon.

Using these possible "setups" (such as a homeless person living in an alley or a character who is a drug addict) you could quite effectively use tuberculosis in your plot. Tuberculosis, also known as "the white plague," would cause symptoms such as weight loss and general wasting, chronic cough, sweats, and general debilitation—possibly even causing the victim to be bedridden.

Other scourges from the past that are returning include **cholera**, measles, syphilis, gonorrhea, hepatitis and malaria.

Cholera

Cholera is epidemic in Latin America and, in just the first six months of 1991, caused more than three thousand deaths. Poverty, crowding, lack of good sanitation and poor health policies gave rise to the recent epidemic of cholera. The conditions in Latin America now are similar to those of London in the 1800s, when more than twenty thousand people died from the disease. According to a report in *Newsweek* of May 6, 1991, the Pan-American Health Organization (PAHO) said that unless drastic measures are taken to curb it, cholera could spread to the entire continent of South America and kill more than forty thousand people over the next three years. Intense nausea and diarrhea are the main symptoms, and it kills quickly, often within twelve hours or less.

Cholera is caused by bacteria and occurs when infected excrement contaminates drinking water or infects seafood that is then ingested by the victim. The bacteria grow in the intestines, and produce a toxin that causes massive diarrhea, vomiting and bleeding. A cholera patient may lose four gallons or more of fluid during the first few hours; victims appear to "shrink" rapidly due to the massive loss of water, and they die quickly from dehydration. Raw fish may also carry the disease from contaminated water. There have been several reported cases of cholera in the United States, both from travelers who brought it back with them, and from imported fruits, vegetables and seafood. Cholera can be prevented by boiling drinking water and cooking all seafood thoroughly. I've concentrated on tuberculosis and cholera here because they are the most rapidly expanding of the ancient "plagues" at this time.

AIDS

AIDS is a new epidemic that has had devastating effects worldwide, with the largest number of cases occurring in countries with poverty, overcrowding and limited medical treatment. AIDS (Acquired Immune Deficiency Syndrome) is caused by the human immunodeficiency virus (HIV). The exact number of cases is not known because of underreporting in central Africa, where it is most prevalent; the official cause of deaths reported is actually from opportunistic infection, and is not reported as a complication of HIV infection.

Brain Injury and Disability

It may serve your story to have a character who is physically disabled. The following section will give you some ideas to consider.

Stroke

If you wish to severely limit a character, a stroke will provide a variety of handicaps. A stroke is an **infarction** (death of tissue) of a part of the brain due to occlusion of blood supply. The more accurate term is cerebral vascular accident, also called a CVA. Symptoms from a stroke depend on the size and the region of the brain that is affected. Following a stroke, a person could be: left speechless but still able to hear and understand; paralyzed on one side of the body and possibly confined to bed or to a wheelchair; able to speak but only with slurring; or left with no awareness of their surroundings, in an almost semivegetative state.

Risk Factors for Stroke

- People fifty-five or older.
- Most common in men, but the risk for women increases after age sixty-five.

- Diabetes.
- Hypertension.
- Heart Disease.
- Smoking.
- Illicit drug use, especially I.V. drug use.

Symptoms of Stroke

- Sudden weakness or numbness of the face, arm or leg on one side of the body. Some people complain of their affected side feeling "heavy" or "dead."
- Loss of speech or trouble talking or understanding speech. This might include slurred speech, inability to speak, or difficulty understanding others.
- Dimness or loss of vision, particularly in one eye. People feel like a "shade has come down" over one eye.
- Unexplained dizziness.
- Severe, sudden headache, possibly with a stiff neck.

Slurred speech, and a numbness or weakness on one side of the body are classic early signs of stroke. If the stroke is large, affecting a significant portion of the brain, the person may become immediately comatose; this may be followed by death if the stroke is severe enough, or there may be only a limited recovery leaving the person with a severe disability: paralysis of one side of the body, speechlessness, limited cognitive ability to speak and to understand others, or being left in a permanent semivegetative state.

Summary of Complications After Stroke

- Collapse with sudden death.
- Permanent coma.
- Partial recovery with a deficit, such as paralysis, inability to speak, inability to reason.
- Rarely, there may be recovery with little or no *visible* deficits.

Severe Head Trauma

Severe head trauma is also common and may be similar to stroke in symptoms and severity. Severe head injury is the leading cause of death for people under the age of forty-five. The survivors may be left with permanent disability that includes memory loss of varying severity, decreased intelligence and paralysis involving one side of the body.

In *Lonesome Dove*, Larry McMurtry uses chronic brain disability very skillfully. Clara's husband, Bob, was kicked in the head by a horse and left an invalid. He hadn't died, but he hadn't recovered. His eyes were open, but he could neither speak nor move. He could swallow, but he was barely alive three months after the accident. He had no control of his bladder or bowels, and Clara had to move and clean the heavy 200-pound man daily.

All of this detail regarding Bob's debility sets the stage for the relationship between Clara and her old lover, Gus.

When Gus finally meets Clara, again, and sees the burden that her invalid husband has become to her, he refuses to have his gangrenous leg amputated — a stubborn act that costs him his life.

> Augustus looked sweaty and unsteady, but the range was short. "Not to kill," Augustus said. "But I'll promise to disable you if you don't let me be about this leg."
>
> "I never took you for a suicide, Gus," Call said. "Men have gotten by without legs. Lots of 'em lost legs in the war. You don't like to do nothing but sit on the porch and drink whiskey anyway. It don't take legs to do that."
>
> "Clara's got one invalid already, and she's bored with him," Augustus said.
>
> Larry McMurtry, *Lonesome Dove* (Pocket)
> — Winner of Pulitzer Prize

By bringing an invalid into the story, McMurtry was able to create empathy for Clara, and a reason for Gus to risk his life so that he too wouldn't become a burden. And notice how McMurtry pulled it off without going into the whys and hows of Bob's injury; rather, he merely stated his disabilities and the burden they caused to Clara, who had to care for him.

Viral Encephalitis

The headline, "Lethal virus in *Awakenings* may be waiting to strike again," appeared in newspapers recently. In the book (and film) *Awakenings*, by Oliver Sacks, people were infected with a virus that swept the world in 1917, affecting more than five million people and killing one-half million before suddenly disappearing. Those people who didn't die immediately became catatonic.

But according to some health experts, the killer virus could surface again. "It happened once, it can happen again," said one of the physicians studying the disease. The virus may return in a more lethal form and strike again. It causes a sleeping sickness called *encephalitis lethargica*. In addition to causing a catatonic statue-like state as depicted in the movie, it drove some people to murder, to manic destructiveness and to suicide.

Using something like the virus mentioned above, you could have a character in a permanent state of catatonia.

Coma

A coma is a deep state of unconsciousness from which the person cannot be aroused; it is usually the result of injury of the brain, disease or poison (or drug induced).

A coma may be a useful tool when you need to have a character either suddenly return to the conscious world after a long absence, or you may wish to put a character into a coma, a gray zone between life and death. The time of the coma can be anything you choose it to be. A coma may last from several hours to years.

In California, a young woman fell into a five-week coma following the birth of twin girls; she was given only a one-percent chance of survival, but came out of her coma in time to spend Christmas with her new family. At the end of her pregnancy, she had developed toxemia; her liver ruptured, her kidneys shut down, her lungs flooded and she bloated more than one hundred pounds from additional fluid.

In Missouri, a woman spent more than two years in a coma, the result of complications following surgery to repair a ruptured artery in her brain. She said she just woke up one day, remembering little more than vivid dreams of repeated attempts to find her way back home.

Harvard law professor Alan Dershowitz wrote about the coma of Sunny von Bulow, wife of Claus von Bulow, in his book *Reversal of Fortune*. In December 1980, Sunny went into a coma and has remained so until this day. Her husband was charged with attempted murder for causing an insulin-induced coma. However, the original verdict of guilty was overturned after a retrial.

Summary

You can see that chronic illness has been used much more extensively than sudden death by writers. Here is a quick summary of the types of chronic illnesses and disabilities that several authors have employed.

Tuberculosis (consumption)	*Camille* by Alexandre Dumas *La Traviata* by Verdi *La Bohème* by Puccini *Long Day's Journey into Night* by Eugene O'Neill
Leprosy	*Ben Hur* by Lew Wallace *Hawaii* by James Michener
Leukemia	*Love Story* by Erich Segal *Dying Young* by Marti Leimbach
Tumorous abdomens, cancer	*Ironweed* by William Kennedy *The Good Earth* by Pearl S. Buck *Terms of Endearment* by Larry McMurtry *Devil's Advocate* by Morris West *Cat on a Hot Tin Roof* by Tennessee Williams *The Shootist* by Glendan Swarthout *Dark Victory* (screenplay, starring Bette Davis, and later version with Elizabeth Montgomery)
Brain damage and stroke	*Lonesome Dove* by Larry McMurtry
Encephalitis from virus	*Awakenings* by Oliver Sacks (a true account)
Gangrene	*Lonesome Dove* by Larry McMurtry
Diabetes mellitus	*Steel Magnolias* by Robert Harling

Childbirth fever	*Our Town* by Thornton Wilder
	Gone With the Wind by Margaret Mitchell
Syphilis	*Of Human Bondage* by Somerset Maugham
Viral Myocarditis	*Beaches* by Iris Dart

This chapter by no means contains an exhaustive list of every chronic disease. In fact, any disease well researched may be used if it suits the needs of both the plot and the character.

Here are some scenarios you might consider for your story:

- A mother of five dies after a complicated delivery. While she lies dying, she talks to her eight-year-old daughter and tells her she must now run the household. The burden of responsibility overwhelms her and years later she ends up in a mental hospital after abusing drugs and attempting suicide.

- An idealistic young Jesuit priest is assigned to an impoverished inner-city parish. He contracts tuberculosis and dies a slow, lingering death while he tries to figure out why God would allow this to happen to him.

- A renowned opera singer has a mild stroke that leaves her with slurred speech. She can never sing again and is filled with despair, but with her keen sense of sound and pitch, discovers she can write music.

As this chapter has shown, chronic illness, coma or slow death can have a profound effect on your characters and provide a great opportunity for change.

T W E L V E

CONTROVERSIES INVOLVING DEATH

Emotionally Induced Death and Voodoo

It is possible for a person to become scared and weak with fear, almost to the point of death. This is not the same kind of fear one has when standing in front of an audience with trembling voice and knocking knees; that is an adrenaline rush. Rather, it is a cold, dark fear that can actually paralyze a person.

After experiencing sudden fear, psychological stress or tremendous pain, the person breaks into a cold sweat, turns pale, loses blood pressure, then may drop to the floor unconscious.

The scenario described is due to the vaso-vagal reaction and is evoked by great emotional stress associated with fear or pain. It is a transient vascular and neurogenic reaction (mediated by the nervous system); marked by pallor (paleness); nausea; cold, clammy sweating; bradycardia (slow heart rate) and a rapid fall in blood pressure that may lead to unconsciousness.

The large blood vessels inside the abdomen dilate and the

blood volume is shunted to the major organs. Peripheral vessels to the arms and legs constrict to compensate, and the patient becomes cold, shakes and is covered with sweat. This vaso-vagal reaction accounts for "sudden death" in the practice of voodoo and witchcraft when curses are placed on the victim. It is actually their own body's response to fear that causes the death they dreaded.

The Journal of the American Medical Association (JAMA) reported on the connection between stress and life-threatening arrhythmias (abnormal, irregular rhythm) of the heart. Some individuals are at high risk of sudden death following stress. There is a clear connection between emotional stress and cardiac vulnerability; this explains why an individual may drop dead from "shock" when told of some family tragedy. There is a similar connection between emotional stress and "voodoo death," where fear and terror are the contributors.

One morning, a Biami tribesman in Papua, New Guinea, who had been in excellent health, believed that some evil sorcery had been cast on him and, thoroughly convinced that it was time to die, he lay down on a rough-hewn mat to wait. By the end of the day he was dead.

The following article appeared in the *Miami Herald*:

HEALTHY ASIAN MEN DIE UNEXPECTEDLY; REASON IS UNCLEAR

It seems right out of a Freddie Krueger horror movie, complete with ghastly nightmares, murderous demons and scores of bodies.

All of the victims are Asian men, typically in their 30's. They have strong physiques and no known ailments. One night they head off to bed and fall asleep. Then in the early morning darkness, something awful happens.

The sleeping men utter agonizing groans and begin to writhe and gasp. It often looks as if they've convulsed with a terrible dream. Within minutes, they are dead. The phenomenon is known as the "nightmare death."

The article goes on to state that over the past decade, scores of such cases have been reported in the United States. Hundreds of similar deaths have also been noted in other parts of the world.

As of yet, no one can say for sure what is killing them.

Some have chalked the deaths up to voodoo curses, while others have blamed vindictive, supernatural forces. Blaming female spirits for the killings, the men have begun wearing dresses and red nail polish to fool the spirits into thinking they're women.

But the deaths continue. Autopsies show no sign of anything that could have killed them.

Voodoo practitioners use both spells and poisons to control, cure or kill their victims. Some of the poisons and "medicines" used include toads, bones, plants, lizards and sea worms. But in a closed system of beliefs as strong as voodoo, the mind may in fact be the strongest drug of all. Death comes from a lethal dose of fear!

The Near-Death Experience

There is another gray area concerning death that has given rise to religious, philosophical and scientific debate. That is the **near-death experience** (NDE) — also called the "Lazarus Syndrome," referring to the biblical Lazarus rising from the dead. Near-death experience is a phrase first coined by Raymond A. Moody in 1975, but NDEs have been reported throughout history by the Greeks, Romans and Egyptians; there are several accounts of it in the Bible as well.

A man is dying and as he reaches the point of greatest physical distress he hears himself pronounced dead by his doctor. There is an utterly black, dark void and he feels himself moving rapidly through a long, dark tunnel. He finds himself outside of his own physical body. He experiences a bright light, a feeling of warmth, peace and quiet, and he sees relatives and friends who have already died, a warm, loving experience of a kind he has never known before.

The bliss that people experience when death approaches has been described by a growing number of people who have "died" (which is to say that their heartbeat and breathing stopped) and have then been revived. The prevailing emotion they describe is euphoria; their flirtation with death is so blissful that they often ask, "Why did you bring me back, Doctor?"

Some physicians have suggested that it is nothing more than the effect of hypoxia (decreased oxygen supply) on the temporal lobe of the brain, while others believe that it is a glance forward into that unknown realm of death.

Carl Sagan, in his book *Broca's Brain*, believes that the NDE is latent memories from birth:

The only alternative, so far as I can see, is that every human being, without exception, has already shared an experience like that of those travelers who return from the land of death; the sensation of flight; the emergence from darkness into light; an experience in which, at least perceived, bathed in radiance and glory. There is only one common experience that matches this description. It is called birth.

There are experiences common to those who have been near death. Raymond A. Moody detailed the near-death experience in his book *The Light Beyond*, and it includes the following:

EXPERIENCE	PERCENT
Out of body	26
Accurate visual perception	23
Audible voices and sounds	17
Feeling of peace	32
Light phenomena	14
Life review	32
Being in another world	32
Encountering other beings	23
Tunnel experience	9
Precognition	6

What do these experiences mean? Do they foretell what death itself is like? Or are the experiences merely a part of the dying process, just a quirk of the human brain that mercifully creates "good feelings" as it becomes anoxic and dies?

Melvin Morse, M.D., in his book *Closer to the Light*, describes the near-death experience in dozens of young children that he interviewed in the hospital. The accounts of their NDE's are identical. Over one hundred children, ages three to nine, who had suffered near-fatal trauma or clinical death during surgery were interviewed, and all reported the same experiences as did adults. Since the children were too young to be influenced by religious teaching or to have formed preconceived ideas of death, the meaning of the near-death experience becomes that much more intriguing.

Choosing a Quiet Death

The list of ways that people die is endless, but most people tend to ignore the reality and presume that they will die in their sleep. Unfortunately, people don't get to choose how they will die (except with suicide).

Many people believe that society has mismanaged dying; most people would like to die a quiet, dignified death, a reasonable wish that is almost never fulfilled. Most people still die in hospitals, where respirators, dialysis machines, nasogastric tubes, endless chemotherapy and cardiopulmonary resuscitation change death into a mechanized spectacle.

While we hope for the best concerning our own death, many people have a fear of the worst, a fear that has given rise to the concept of a **living will**. This is a document designed to give people more control over their dying and to prevent them from being kept in a vegetative state by mechanical devices.

The real issue is that we can't really come to grips with our own death, that moment when we no longer exist. The old and sick may know how they'll die, but even they aren't usually ready to come to terms with death.

> *Do not go gentle into that good night,*
> *Old age should burn and rave at close of day;*
> *Rage, rage against the dying of the light.*
>
> Dylan Thomas, "Do Not Go Gentle Into That Good Night"

There are many conflicting attitudes toward death and dying. Complex issues come into play, such as terminally ill individuals who struggle to survive at any cost versus those who search for a quick and easy death. Both groups often find themselves in conflict with family members, clergy, religious beliefs and the law.

The court may try to prevent someone from being taken off life-support, or a lawyer may lobby for euthanasia; clergy may encourage the dying not to give in to suicide since only God can give or take life; family members may not want to give up a loved one, or may seek means to help them end their life of pain.

Emotional and Ethical Problems Related to Death

Cryonics

"It's not that I want to come back. It's that I don't want to die."
That's how a woman, who is a member of the Immortalist Society,
described her interest in cryonics.

Through the ages, people have tried to come up with new ideas
to prevent or postpone the inevitable—*death*. One of the more intriguing and unusual methods is freezing your body in a vat of liquid
nitrogen at -270° Fahrenheit in the hopes of being thawed out to
live again sometime in the future.

Cryonics is the freezing of a person's body at the time of legal
death with the intent to be thawed and revived in the future when
a cure for the disease or ailment is found. People who believe in
cryonics hope that a nap in deep freeze will save them from death.
One officer from the Cryonics Institute said, "We're not a bunch of
fanatics waiting to plunge into nitrogen. No one is ever sure if it's
totally reversible."

A man in California failed to persuade a Superior Court judge
to let him freeze his head before he is pronounced legally dead from
a brain tumor. "There's a public relations problem involved in heads
only, so we avoid it," one of the members of the Cryonics Institute
explained.

People magazine reported a story about the death of actor Dick
Clair who was determined not to let the grim reaper have the last
laugh. Clair's mortal remains are preserved in super-cold storage. If
everything goes according to plan, Clair "has not entered The Big
Sleep, but merely a Long Nap." He believed he might someday be
thawed, cured, revived and returned to the world of the living.

Moments after Clair died, his body was packed in crushed ice,
and his blood drained and replaced with a cryo-agent. Liquid nitrogen was then sprayed into a giant Thermos bottle, chilling the body
to a final temperature of -320° Fahrenheit.

But those who knew him say death scored its real victory over
him while he was still very much alive. He always worried about the
future, about living forever. Now he lies frozen in a giant Thermos
bottle—not exactly a victor over the grim reaper after all.

This concept—freezing one's body for centuries, only to be

thawed out sometime in the future — and those who would choose to do this — is great material for the writer to explore.

Hospice

Many people choose to die in the familiar surroundings of their own homes with friends and family at their bedside, instead of in the sterile, busy and unfamiliar environment of the hospital.

Hospice is an organization that was developed to assist those caring for terminally ill family members at home. After the terminally ill person is brought home to die, a nurse from Hospice will make a preliminary visit to answer questions, tell the family what to expect, and give them suggestions and guidelines to help them and the dying. Hospice is "on call" at all times to give comfort or to answer questions and give instructions when necessary.

Hospice is a fantastic program that reaches out to millions of people and households each year. Hospice restores control and dignity to both the dying and their family at a time when everything seems impersonal and regulated.

The Right-to-Die and Euthanasia

At the opposite end of the spectrum from those who fight for immortality are those who seek an easy way to end life's struggle.

To them, merely staying alive is not the best choice when faced with constant pain or physical/mental disabilities, and suicide or assisted death seems like the only way out of a hopeless situation. Recent cases such as those involving Nancy Cruzan, Karen Ann Quinlan, Roswell Gilbert and Janet Adkins have forced the right-to-die question into the open.

The "right to die" seems like a ridiculous term since death is so inevitable. But as humans we simply cannot accept death easily and fight to keep others alive at all cost, regardless of *their* desires. Yet suicide is against the law and considered a sin by most religions. We struggle to understand and conquer death, but we cannot.

Dr. Jack Kevorkian, a retired pathologist from Michigan, began working on a suicide machine after meeting a quadriplegic who had to go to court to get permission to have his own ventilator turned off. Dr. Kevorkian, a longtime advocate of euthanasia, wanted the medical and legal establishment to consider the rights of others to choose to die peacefully, when and how they wish. "My ultimate aim is to make euthanasia a positive experience."

Dr. Kevorkian's suicide machine releases sodium pentathol

through an intravenous tube; sixty seconds later, when the person is utterly unconscious, a timer triggers a second switch to release potassium chloride into the system, which, when it reaches the heart, immediately stops it. It promises a swift, painless death.

While some argue that it is *too* user-friendly, that it makes suicide too easy, too accessible, too imaginable; Kevorkian argues that the real issue is that it forces people to face their own mortality, and stirs up questions they don't want to face. While the Dutch have a euthanasia program in which terminally ill patients can get a lethal injection from their doctors, some medical ethicists argue that the medical profession should not be involved in assisting suicide.

Kevorkian believes that it is cruel and barbaric to keep people alive who must live with horrible intractable pain, and feels that doctors have not learned to deal with the agony of the dying.

When a woman with an incurable disease came to him because she didn't want to suffer, he hooked her up to his suicide machine. She pushed the button and released potassium chloride into her veins. Just before she died, she looked up at Kevorkian with grateful eyes and said, "Thank you, thank you, thank you."

Kevorkian months later assisted two more women with their suicides. Some consider him a hero who helped those suffering end their misery with dignity. But his critics call him a villain; dubbing him a "serial mercy killer." At the very least, Dr. Kevorkian is forcing society to look at a complex problem, to face questions that need answers.

Dr. Timothy Quill helped a terminally ill woman die because she was facing a painful, agonizing death. He said, "I have been a longtime advocate of a patient's right to die with as much control and dignity as possible."

It was clear to Dr. Quill that the woman knew what she was doing and that she was sad and frightened to be leaving, but that she would be even more terrified to stay and suffer. He suggested that she contact the Hemlock Society, an organization that advocates the right of the terminally ill to commit suicide.

"To think that people do not suffer in the process of dying is an illusion," Dr. Quill said.

When her disease progressed to a stage that she could no longer bear, he provided her with a prescription for barbiturates, along with instructions on what dosage would be fatal. "She taught me about life, death and honesty, and about taking charge and facing tragedy squarely when it strikes."

He added sadly, "I wonder whether she struggled in that last hour, and whether the Hemlock Society's way of death by suicide is the most benign. I wonder why she, who gave so much to so many of us, had to be alone for the last hour of her life."

Nancy Cruzan was another landmark right-to-die case. Cruzan, age thirty-three, had been in a persistent vegetative state since a 1983 car accident. A judge granted her parents permission to disconnect her feeding tube.

But the day her feeding tube was to be disconnected, nineteen right-to-life protesters were arrested trying to reach her hospital room to prevent it. "She's going to be dead soon, if someone doesn't intervene," said one of the protesters. "Citizens have to stop standing by silently and letting people die."

Many less dramatic day-to-day decisions are made by physicians and family members to allow patients near death to die, cases that never make the headlines.

Derek Humphry founded the National Hemlock Society after he helped his wife of twenty-two years end her struggle with an inoperable cancer. He has written several books, the latest titled *Final Exit: The Practicalities of Self-Deliverance and Assisted Suicide for the Dying* that contains how-to information on suicide.

Living Wills

Rose Gasner, director of legal services of the Society for the Right-to-Die, says most people want control over their fate. There are three main variations of right-to-die laws:

Living Will: Allows individuals to specify in writing their wishes regarding life-prolonging treatment.

Durable Power of Attorney: allows individuals to designate another person to make medical decisions for them.

Statutory Surrogate Provision: Authorizes certain individuals, such as a spouse or court-appointed guardian, to decide for the patient, if the wishes have not been specified in writing.

A copy of a Living Will is included here, printed with permission of the Society for the Right-to-Die, 250 West 57th Street, New York, NY 10107.

A Living Will is an example of an instructional advance direc-

Society for the Right to Die

250 West 57th Street/New York, NY 10107

Living Will Declaration

INSTRUCTIONS
Consult this column for guidance.

To My Family, Doctors, and All Those Concerned with My Care

I. _____, being of sound mind, make this statement as a directive to be followed if I become unable to participate in decisions regarding my medical care.

This declaration sets forth your directions regarding medical treatment.

If I should be in an incurable or irreversible mental or physical condition with no reasonable expectation of recovery, I direct my attending physician to withhold or withdraw treatment that merely prolongs my dying. I further direct that treatment be limited to measures to keep me comfortable and to relieve pain.

You have the right to refuse treatment you do not want, and you may request the care you do want.

These directions express my legal right to refuse treatment. Therefore I expect my family, doctors, and everyone concerned with my care to regard themselves as legally and morally bound to act in accord with my wishes, and in so doing to be free of any legal liability for having followed my directions.

You may list specific treatment you do not want. For example:
  Cardiac resuscitation
  Mechanical respiration
  Artificial feeding/fluids by tube
Otherwise, your general statement, top right, will stand for your wishes.

I especially do not want: _____
_____
_____
_____
_____

You may want to add instructions or care you do want—for example, pain medication; or that you prefer to die at home if possible.

Other instructions/comments: _____
_____
_____

Proxy Designation Clause: Should I become unable to communicate my instructions as stated above, I designate the following person to act in my behalf:

If you want, you can name someone to see that your wishes are carried out, but you do not have to do this.

Name _____
Address _____

If the person I have named above is unable to act on my behalf, I authorize the following person to do so:

Name _____
Address _____

This Living Will Declaration expresses my personal treatment preferences. The fact that I may have also executed a document in the form recommended by state law should not be construed to limit or contradict this Living Will Declaration, which is an expression of my common-law and constitutional rights.

Sign and date here in the presence of two adult witnesses, who should also sign.

Signed: _____ Date: _____
Witness: _____ Witness: _____
Address: _____ Address: _____

Keep the signed original with your personal papers at home. Give signed copies to doctors, family, and proxy. Review your Declaration from time to time; initial and date it to show it still expresses your intent.

Sample living will.

tive in which you instruct others on how you want your care handled; a Durable Power of Attorney for health care is an example of a proxy advance directive giving others the authority to direct your care.

In Minneapolis, a man is fighting with doctors because he refuses to let his wife die. The doctors say that while such sentiment may seem heroic, it isn't helping anyone, including his wife, who has been in a coma for seventeen months. The doctors want him replaced as his wife's legal guardian because he refuses to let them unplug the respirator that keeps her breathing.

The doctors say he just doesn't understand that his wife is in a persistent vegetative state. The case is believed to be the first in the country in which doctors have gone against the wishes of a family in an attempt to terminate life-sustaining medical care.

But a member of the Anti-Euthanasia Task Force argues, "We've heard over and over that families should decide, and now doctors are saying there ought to be limits."

The National Hemlock Society, The Society for the Right-to-Die, the Anti-Euthanaisa Task Force, The Cryogenics Society and supporters of the suicide machine confront each other daily, looking for answers where there are none, looking for truth where there is no absolute truth.

How You Might Use This Material

For you as a writer, these emotional issues surrounding death and dying that are filled with conflict make fertile ground for plot. You may choose to write about the internal conflict the dying person experiences, whether to end it quickly or struggle at all costs to survive. Or, you may focus your story on the problems that caregivers must face; these can include the clergy, nurses and doctors, as well as family members. Here are some scenarios you might consider for your story:

- A mother can't bear to allow doctors to turn off the respirator that keeps her little boy alive, while she clings to a fragment of hope.

- A lawyer sees his elderly mother tormented as doctors and nurses struggle to keep her alive; it is against the law in his state to order withdrawal of life support, and to do so might be considered murder and result in his disbarrment.

- A nurse gives a fatal dose of morphine to a suffering young woman with a terminal disease, and is charged with murder. (See *Fatal Dosage* by Gary Provost.)

- A wife, the only person who knows of a second will that leaves the vast majority of her husband's estate to charity, moves ahead quickly through the courts to withdraw life support from him and "allow the man she loves to die in peace." For her the motive is greed; the act is murder.

And so the struggle of life and death continues in a war with no victors. We fight against death, against that day when life will be smothered out by a dark nothingness. We hope to have a say as to how we die by inventing "living wills." We read magazines like *Longevity, Prevention, Health, American Health, In Health* and *Men's Health*. We smear on anti-aging creams, gulp down vitamins and think up new and inventive exercises.

But death always wins.

Glossary

A-/AN-: Means without or absence. For example, anoxia means lack of oxygen; asystole means absence of systole (a heartbeat).

ANOXIA: Complete absence of oxygen.

APNEA: Absence of breathing. Apnea is one of the two signs of clinical death. The other is absent pulse.

ARTERIOSCLEROTIC: Degenerative changes of arteries, primarily to heart and brain, characterized by thickening and hardening of the artery wall. This causes decreased blood flow.

ASPHYXIATION: Death due to anoxia, or lack of oxygen.

ASYSTOLE: Complete absence of heartbeat.

ATTENDED DEATH: A death that is witnessed by a physician. An unattended death is one without a physician present, and requires a ruling by the coroner.

AUTOPSY: The postmortem dissection and examination of the body. There are two types, medical autopsy—done to establish the medical cause of death, and medical-legal autopsy, to establish the legal cause of death, usually in cases of suspicious death.

BRADYCARDIA: Abnormally slow heartbeat, usually a pulse less than sixty.

BRAIN DEATH: See *Death*.

CAFE CORONARY: A death caused by choking on food lodged in the throat (obstructing air in the trachea). So named because it resembles a heart attack and happens while eating.

CASE FILE: A large 12 × 14-inch envelope that contains the paperwork, photographs, legal identification records, fingerprint cards and autopsy report along with the opinion, which become police property.

CAUSE OF DEATH: The physical event or object that brought about the death of a person (gunshot, heart attack, electrocution).

CHEST TUBE: A large-bore catheter placed in the chest, between the lung and chest wall, to remove any accumulated air and fluid.

CHOLERA: An acute infectious disease caused by bacteria; symptoms include diarrhea, nausea and vomiting, and fluid loss with dehydration, and results in rapid death.

CLINICAL DEATH: See *Death*.

CODE: Usually *CODE-99* or *CODE-BLUE*; a coded message to alert the attending medical staff of a cardiac arrest and to instigate an immediate response for resuscitation.

COMA: A state of unconsciousness from which the patient cannot be aroused, even by painful stimuli.

CONSUMPTION: An old term for tuberculosis; an infection that affects mainly the lungs, but may also attack the brain, bones, kidneys and other organs. Causes a slow, debilitating and chronic death.

CORONER: An elected official who must investigate the circumstances surrounding the cause of death. Most coroners today are trained forensic pathologists, but that is not a prerequisite in all states and counties yet. See *Medical Examiner*.

CORPUS DELICTI: (Body of Evidence) All the evidence that has been obtained regarding a crime (usually a murder).

CPR: Cardiopulmonary resuscitation. A mechanical method of maintaining air to the lungs and compressing the heart to move blood, usually a temporary means of sustaining life until further medical treatment can be started. ABC's are Airway, Breathing and Circulation.

CREMAINS: The bone fragments and ashes remaining after cremation, which are usually pulverized into small granular particles and added to the ashes.

CREMATION: Reduction of the body to ashes by use of a very hot furnace, 1800° F or hotter.

CRYONICS: The deep-freezing of human bodies at death for preservation and possible revival in the future.

CT SCAN: Also called "CAT" scan, meaning Computerized Axial Tomography. A machine used to obtain axial images of the body using X rays to produce a composite 3-D picture. From this, individual "slices" may be viewed on a screen, revealing internal structures more clearly than normal X rays.

CVA: Cerebral vascular accident. A stroke, meaning that part of the brain has died due to blockage of blood vessels.

CYANOTIC: From "cyano" meaning blue. Cyanosis is a bluish discoloration of skin due to lack of oxygen.

DEATH: The permanent cessation of all vital functions in a living organism. **CLINICAL DEATH:** Absence of breathing (apnea) and heartbeat (asystole). This stage is survivable with prompt resuscitation efforts. **BRAIN DEAD** (and **MEDICAL-LEGAL DEATH**): Death where all cerebral (brain) function has ceased.

DEATH CERTIFICATE: A legal document that must be completed by a physician or coroner, giving the exact cause of death. This must be signed before burial or cremation can occur.

DEFIBRILLATOR: A machine used to treat fibrillation of the heart and restore normal rhythmic contractions by application of electrical impulses to the heart through paddles placed over the chest wall.

D.O.A.: Dead on Arrival at the hospital or medical facility.

DURABLE POWER OF ATTORNEY: Allows individuals to specify in writing their wishes regarding life-prolonging treatment. See also *Living Will*.

EMBALMING: To inject a body with chemicals to retard decay. Embalming is *not* required by law in any state.

EMS: Emergency Medical System. A medical emergency transportation system established to get an injured person to a medical facility as quickly as possible, and to provide medical assistance during transportation.

EN BLOC: In a lump; as a whole. For instance, the intestines might be removed en bloc (or all together as a single unit).

ENDOTRACHEAL TUBE: Meaning "within the trachea"; it is a large tube passed into the trachea, usually to maintain respiration by mechanical device.

FALL: There are two types of falls: **CONTROLLED FALL:** Landing on both feet. With a controlled fall, survival is possible with falls up to and exceeding 100 vertical feet. **UNCONTROLLED FALL:** Landing on part of the body other than the feet; death may result from even very short falls of 15- to 20-foot heights.

FIXED LIVIDITY: See *Lividity* and *Livor Mortis*.

FORENSIC PATHOLOGIST: A pathologist with special training into the medical-legal investigation of circumstances surrounding a death, usually a medical examiner or coroner.

FUNERAL HOME: After the body has been identified, and the Death Certificate signed listing the cause of death, the body is taken to a funeral home to prepare for burial or cremation. This is where embalming is performed (if elected to do so).

HEIMLICH MANEUVER: Also called *the abdominal thrust*. It consists of standing behind a choking victim, making a fist with both hands, and thrusting in and upwards beneath the ribcage to force air out of the lungs and dislodge the obstruction.

HEMOLYTIC (HEMOLYSIS): The release of hemoglobin from the red blood cells. In effect, it is the disintegration of red blood cells.

HOSPICE: An organization to assist the family in caring for a terminally ill person at home, and to lend assistance during death and dying in the home.

HYPO: Deficient. Thus, hypoxia means deficient oxygen; contrast that to anoxia, which means complete lack of oxygen.

HYPOTENSION: Low blood pressure.

INFARCTION (INFARCT): An area of tissue death and necrosis due to lack of blood supply of oxygen.

INTUBATE: To insert a tube.

JAUNDICED: A yellow color to the skin caused by the deposition of bilirubin or bile pigment in the skin. This is usually caused by bile obstruction or advanced liver disease.

KAROSHI: A term used by the Japanese to describe a form of sudden death from a heart attack, usually attributed to stress from working too hard.

LEGAL TIME OF DEATH: The time that the body is first discovered is recorded as the legal time of death. The legal time of death for a body that has been dead for days or weeks is the time that it is first discovered (not the time of actual death).

LIVIDITY: The discoloration (a purplish "liver" color to a greenish color) caused from blood settling down to the dependant parts of a dead body. **FIXED LIVIDITY:** Occurs after six to eight hours, and means the blood has coagulated and will not redistribute if the body is turned over, and will not blanch with pressure.

LIVING WILL: Allows individuals to specify in writing their wishes regarding life-prolonging treatment.

LIVOR MORTIS: Same as *Lividity*. Liver-red discoloration, as above.

MANNER OF DEATH: The means of death. There are four possible manners of death: natural causes, homicide, suicide and accident.

MEDICAL EXAMINER: A pathologist with special training in forensic medicine, to investigate and determine the cause of death. While a coroner is an elected official, the medical examiner is usually hired by the county or city to investigate the medical-legal cause of death. For all practical purposes, coroner and medical examiner are similar titles, and usually have the same degree of training.

MI (MYOCARDIAL INFARCTION): The correct medical term for heart attack. A portion of the heart muscle dies because of blockage of one or more coronary arteries.

MORGUE: A place where dead bodies are kept, usually in refrigeration, for identification, until an autopsy is performed, or until claimed for burial. It is the place where the autopsy is performed.

MRI SCAN (MAGNETIC RESONANCE IMAGING): One of the newer types of medical imaging. It performs scans similar to CT scans, but uses a powerful magnet instead of X rays to generate images of the body.

NEAR-DEATH EXPERIENCE (NDE): A common group of experiences reported by people who have had clinical death that was reversed: out-of-body sensation; a feeling of peace; light phenomena within a tunnel; precognition; and encountering other deceased individuals.

NECROSIS: Death of tissue, usually as cells in a localized area.

NEUROGENIC: Originating in the nervous system. A neurogenic process or disease would involve the nervous system, brain and spinal cord.

OPINION: The statement at the conclusion of the medical-legal autopsy that gives the nature of the injury, the cause of death, and any other factor that is pertinent.

PACEMAKER: An electrical device to regulate heart rate, consisting of a battery (usually lithium) and a wire to give ryhthmic electric pulses to the heart.

PARAMEDIC: A trained person who works within the EMS system to deliver emergency care and transportation of an individual to a medical facility.

PETECHIAE: Small pinpoint hemorrhages; these can occur around the mouth, eyes and face due to increased pressure, usually from strangulation.

PNEUMOTHORAX: Accumulation of air in the space between the lung and the chest wall. The air pocket compresses the lung and prevents it from expanding and exchanging oxygen properly.

POSTMORTEM: The period after death. A postmortem exam is an examination of the body after death.

RESPIRATOR/VENTILATOR: A mechanical device that maintains respiration by delivering a fixed amount of air at a determined rate.

RIGOR MORTIS: The muscular stiffening of a dead body as a result of depletion of adenosine triphosphate (ATP—the energy source for muscles).

RINGERS LACTATE: An intravenous fluid that contains sodium and potassium, administered to replace lost body fluid.

SALICYLATES: One of the anti-inflammatory group of drugs, such as aspirin.

SHOCK: A critical decrease in blood flow that causes organ damage; usually the result of massive blood loss or dangerously low blood pressure with insufficient profusion of tissues. Symptoms are a feeble pulse, slow respiration, pale color, cold, clammy skin, anxiety, and then unconsciousness.

STATUTORY SURROGATE PROVISION: Authorizes certain individuals, such as a spouse or court-appointed guardian, to decide terminal care for the person, if the patient has not so specified in writing.

STRANGULATION: Closure of blood vessels and air passages of the neck, causing death.

STROKE: A common term for cerebral vascular accident, or CVA, of the brain. A portion of the brain dies (infarcts) due to blockage of blood vessels.

SUBDURAL HEMATOMA (SUBDURAL BLEED): Accumulation of blood or blood clot between the rigid skull and the fleshy brain, causing dangerous compression and displacement of the brain.

SUCKING CHEST WOUND: A hole in the chest wall usually from trauma (gunshot or stabbing); with breathing, air is forced into and out of the chest wall injury.

SUFFOCATION: Death due to failure of oxygen to get to the brain. Not the same as strangulation, since suffocation can be caused by pressure on the chest, which prevents the lungs from moving, or placing an obstruction over the mouth.

TRIAGE: A French word meaning "to sort." New ER patients are triaged to determine the most critical treatment priority.

TUBERCULOSIS (TB): See *Consumption*.

VASO-VAGAL REACTION: *Vaso*—referring to blood vessels; *Vagal*—referring to stimulation of the vagus nerve. This causes dilation of the blood vessels and a drastic drop in blood pressure; the patient is pale, cold, clammy, has a slow heart rate, and may become unconscious. Fear alone can cause a massive vaso-vagal reaction that may result in death in rare instances.

VENTILATOR: See *Respirator*.

VENTRICULAR FIBRILLATION: A twitching or quivering of the heart muscle; it is an ineffective contraction of the heart, with electrical impulses so rapid and erratic that normal coordinated contractions cannot occur. Death results if not treated immediately.

VENTRICULAR TACHYCARDIA: A very rapid heart rate (range of 120 to 140), which by itself is not fatal, but may go directly into a fatal ventricular fibrillation.

VITAL SIGNS: The measurement of heart rate, blood pressure, rate of respiration and temperature.

"Y" INCISION: A two-part incision made on the body during an autopsy. The thoracic-abdominal incision is made across the chest from shoulder to shoulder, crossing down over the breasts; then from the xyphoid process (lower tip of the sternum) a midline incision is extended down the entire length of the abdomen to the pubis.

Bibliography

Books

Carlson, Lisa. *Caring for Your Own Dead*. Hinesburg, Vermont, Upper Access Publishers, 1987. (An excellent handbook describing laws for each state regarding burial, living wills and death certificates. The book details the costs of caskets, burial customs and transporting the dead for burial.)

Clayman, C.B. (ed.). *The American Medical Association Encyclopedia of Medicine*. New York: Random House, 1989. (Authoritative source of information with extensive illustrations, many of them photographs.)

DiMaio, Dominick and Vincent DiMaio. *Forensic Pathology*. New York: Elsevier, 1989. (This textbook is part of Elsevier's series in practical aspects of criminal and forensic investigations. Many photographs included.)

Moody, Raymond, Jr. *The Light Beyond*. New York: Bantam Books, 1988. (Moody has published several books recounting in detail the near-death experience. This is his first, and he goes into some detail on the NDE and also provides several medical possibilities that may account for them.)

Morse, Melvin, M.D., and Paul Perry. *Closer to the Light*. New York: Ivy Books, 1990. (Dr. Morse, a pediatrician, accounts the details of near-death experiences in children.)

Sifakis, Carl. *The Encyclopedia of American Crime*. New York: Facts on File, 1982. (This large, comprehensive book details crimes, prisons, gangsters, criminal techniques, executions and famous trials. It contains over 150 drawings, photographs and illustrations, is well organized and easy to use.)

Spitz and Fisher. *Medicolegal Investigation of Death*. Charles C. Thomas, 1973. (The gold-standard for a textbook on medicolegal aspects of death. Uses photographs, drawings and diagrams liberally throughout; the material is well organized.)

Webster's Medical Desk Dictionary. Springfield, MA: Merriam-Webster, 1986. (Best source for spellings. Emphasizes word definition and usage for those who write about medicine; most other medical dictionaries emphasize diagnosis and treatment for those who practice medicine and nursing.)

Articles

Schrof, Joannie. "Murder They Chirped: Insect detectives are the latest scientific tool in criminal investigation." *U.S. News & World Report*, Oct. 4, 1991.

Index

A

Abdomen injuries, 29, 37, 39
  test for bleeding in, 39
Accident prevention, 164
Accidental death
  in bathrooms, 158
  chances of, 158-159
  among children, 163-164
  from choking, 155
  by electrocution, 159
  from falling, 153-154
  on the farm, 157-158
  from food poisoning, 150-152
  from forceful blow, 156
  from inhalation, 157
  from insect bites, 147-148
  from jellyfish stings, 149
  and left-handed people, 157
  from lightning, 162
  in literature, 142-143, 149
  in nature and outdoors, 148-149
  newspaper accounts of, 144-146
  in plot, 144, 166
  from rabies, 149-150
  in sports, 157
  statistics, 142-166
  in winter, 152-153
  work-related, 157
AIDS, 179
Ambu bag, 37
Anatomical nomenclature, 91
Anoxia, 6
Anticholinergics, 22
Anti-Euthanasia Task Force, 195
Appearance of patient and treatment,
  22-23
Arrhythmias of the heart, 169
Arteriosclerotic coronary artery disease, 169
Asphyxiation
  definition of, 113-114
  by food, 155
  in hanging, 114-115, 116-117
  in poisoning, 115, 118
Assault injury, 39-40
  and dead on arrival, 43
Asystole, 6
Autopsy, 69-93

  case file, 92-93
  for dead on arrival, 43
  of fetus or newborn infant, 89-90
  and identification of body, 73-75
  information determined by, 75-78
  medical-legal, 70-71, 90
  procedure, 73
  protocol, 88-89
  reportable deaths and, 71-72
  room, 77
  ruling on cause of death, 72-73
  step by step, 78-84
  terminology, 91, 92-93

B

Battered wife syndrome, 95
Blood loss, classification of, 26-27
Blood pressure, low, and shock, 27, 29
Body, disposal of, 55-60
  historical and religious background
    and, 55
Bradycardia, 22
Brain death, 3
  criteria for determining, 4
  during emergency resuscitation, 35
  in terminal state, 6
Brain injury and disability, 179-183
  See also Head injury
Bullets
  caliber of, 103-104
  design of, 105-107
  extent of damage by, 103-107
  force of, 109
  muzzle velocity of, 105
  types of, 104
Burial
  customs, 55-56
  regulations, 58-59

C

Cafe Coronary, 155
Cancer, 176
Capital punishment, 123-136
  by electric chair, 132-134
  by firing squad, 130-132
  in gas chamber, 134
  by hanging, 126-130

by lethal injection, 134-136
methods of, 126
Carbon monoxide poisoning, 114,
119-120
Cardiac death, 35
Cardiopulmonary Resuscitation
(CPR), 24
termination of, 35
Cardiovascular system and sudden
death, 171
Case file for legal proceedings, 92-93
CAT scan, 39
Cause of death
accidents as, 142-166
asphyxiation as, 113-114
and autopsy, 75
certification of, 46
among children, 163-164
chronic illness as, 168
disease as, 168, 169, 171
emotional stress as, 185-187
exhumation to determine, 84-87
hanging as, 114-115, 116
and need for privacy, 87-88
poisoning as, 115-120
Cerebral vascular accident. See Stroke
Chemical asphyxiation, 114
Chest, flail, 37
Chest injuries, 29, 36
Chest tube, 36
Chest wound, sucking, 13, 35, 36-37, 38
Child abuse injuries, 40
Childbirth, death from, 174-175
Choking, 155
See also Asphyxiation
Cholera, 178-179
Chronic illness and disease
in literature, 174-177, 181-184
use of, in plot, 168, 174, 177-178, 179,
182, 184
Clinical death, 3, 6
Code in emergency room, 18, 24
Color of patient and diagnosis, 23
Coma, 6, 182-183
Computerized tomography, 39
Consumption. See Tuberculosis
Coroner, 60, 61
and certification of death, 46, 48-51
and DOA, 43, 46
CPR, 24, 35
Cremation, 56-57

Critical treatment priority in emer-
gency room, 18-19
Cryogenics Society, The, 195
Cryonics, 191
CT scan, 39
Cyanosis, 22

D

Dead body
disposal of, 55-60
procedures after discovery of, 52-53
Dead on arrival, 43-44
Deadly Doses, 152
Death
declaration of, 46-48
definition of, 3
in emergency room, 44
emotional problems and, 190-196
ethical problems and, 190-196
manner of, 75, 95-96
mechanism of, 75, 96
procedures followed after, 52-53
reportable, 71-72
sudden, 167-173
time of, 62-68
See also Accidental death, Cause of
death, Dying process
Death certificate, 48-51
Death penalty and executions, 124-125,
136
See also Capital punishment
Defibrillator, 24, 28
Disease as cause of death, 168, 169, 171
See also Chronic illness and disease
DNA analysis, 81, 86
Drowning
in bathtub, 158
childhood, 164
definition of, 110
episode, 11
establishing time of, 111-112
facts regarding, 111
investigation of, 112-113
murder vs. suicide in, 120-121
Drugs, ingestion of, and appearance,
22-23
Dying process, 4-8
terminal state sequence in, 6-8

E

Electrical injuries, 160-162
  and activities of children, 161
  current and, 163
Electrocution, accidental, 159-162
Embalmers, 59-60
Embalming, 57
Emergency case, Bobby Hicks, 10-14, 27, 44
Emergency crash cart, 24-26
Emergency Medical Services System Act, 165
Emergency room
  cases reported to authorities, 39-44
  code, 18
  critical treatment priority, 18-19
  examination in, 19-21
  and the "golden hour," 165-166
  major shock-trauma, 16-17
  standard treatment, 15
  treatment and transportation, 164-166
Emotional problems and death, 190-195
  use of, in plot, 195-196
Emotional stress as cause of death, 185-187
Endotracheal tube, 22
Ethical problems and death, 190-196
Euthanasia, 191-195
Executions, 123-125
  See also Capital punishment

F

Falling as cause of death, 153-154
Fear as cause of death, 185-187
Final Exit, 193
Firearms
  deaths from injuries inflicted by, 98-99
  discharge of, 100
  See also Guns
Food poisoning, 150-152
Forensic anthropology, 86
Forensic entomology, 64
Forensic pathologist, 60, 61
Funeral director, 59-60
Funerals, 57

G

Guns
  discharge of 100, 101, 107
  firing, 99-101
  history of, in America, 98
  See also Bullets, Firearms
Gunshot injury
  as cause of death, 98-99
  damage in, 103-107
  and disability range, 109
  evaluating, 101
  and force of bullet, 109
  in homicide vs. suicide, 107-108, 120
  pain and, 108-109
  survival time with, 108
  See also Gunshot wound
Gunshot wound
  abdominal, 39
  distance estimation of, 101
  and DOA, 43
  entrance of, 101-103
  See also Gunshot injury

H

Hanging, 114-115
  as capital punishment, 126-130
  murder vs. suicide in, 122
Head injury
  death from, 166
  examination of, 30
  from falling, 153
  types of, 29
  See also Brain injury
Heart attack
  appearance of patient with, 22
  and sudden death, 169-172
  and winter, 153
Heimlich maneuver, 155
Hematoma, subdural, 30
Hemlock Society, 192-193, 195
Hemorrhage and blood loss, 26-27
Hicks case, Bobby, 10-14
  autopsy, 76, 89
  shock treatment in, 27
  summary, 44
Homicide vs. suicide,
  factors determining, 120-122
  in gunshot injury, 107-108, 120
  See also Murder
Hospice, 191

Humphry, Derek, 193
Hypotension and blood loss, 26

I

Injury, types of, 29
Instantaneous death, 4-5
Intubation, 22

J

Jaundice, 22

K

"Karoshi," 172
Kevorkian, Dr. Jack, 191-192

L

"Lazarus syndrome." *See* Near-death
        experience
Leukemia, 176
Lightning accidents, 162-163
Living will, 189, 193-195
Lung, collapsed, 36

M

Medical examiner, 60-61
    and DOA, 43
Miscarriage, death from, 175
Morgue, 73-75
Mortician, 59-60
Murder
    by hanging, 117
    by poisoning, 118
    vs. suicide, 107-108, 120-122
Myocardial infarction. *See* Heart attack

N

Near-death experience, 187-189
Neurogenic reaction, 22
"Nightmare death," 186-187
Nonpenetrating injuries, 29, 39

O

Odor of toxins in diagnosis, 23

Opinion in medical-legal autopsy, 73,
        88-89

P

Pacemaker, 7
Pain
    and gunshot injury, 108-109
    reaction to, 185
    and trauma, 30
Penetrating injuries, 29, 39
Pneumothorax, 36, 38
Poisoning, 115-120
    arsenic, 118
    carbon monoxide, 114
    cyanide, 118-119
    Deadly Doses, reference book on, 152
    food, 150-152
    strychnine, 119
Postmortem changes in death process,
        63-68
Pupils
    and brain death, 35
    and drug abuse, 34-35
    examination in diagnosis, 30-36
    size of, 31-33
    and termination of resuscitation,
        35-36

Q

Quill, Dr. Timothy, 192-193

R

Rape case emergency treatment, 41-43
Respirator, 37
Right to die, 191-195
    laws, 193-195
Rigor mortis, 65, 66
    See also Postmortem changes
Ringers lactate, 27

S

Salicylates, 22
Scared to death, 172
Shock
    definition of, 27
    dying in, 5
    signs of, 27

traumatic, 27
treatment for, 27-29
Sleeping sickness. *See* Viral encephalitis
Smell in identifying toxins and diagnosis, 23
Society for the Right-to-Die, 193, 195
Stab wounds, 29, 39
Stabbing in murder vs. suicide, 121-122
State death penalty, 137-140
Strangulation, 22, 114
Stress and sudden death, 186
Stroke, 173, 179-180
Sudden death from natural causes
 common causes of, 170-173
 and coroner, 170
 definition of, 169
 in plot, 167-169, 170, 173
 use of, in literature, 167-169
Suffocation, 114
 See also Asphyxiation
Suicide
 accidental shooting vs., 107
 differences between homicide and, 107-108, 120-122
 facts about, 97
 from gunshot injury, 98
 by hanging, 114-115, 116
 Hemlock Society and, 192-193
 in literature, 96
 methods, 97-98
 in movies, 96
 rate, 96-97
 and right to die, 191-193

T

Terminal stages of life, 6-8

Time of death, 62-68
 estimated, 62, 76
 importance in murder cases, 62
 insects and, 64
 legal, 47
 postmortem changes and, 63-68
 sequential changes to body and, 65-68
 sources used in determining, 63
Toe tag, 74, 75
Toxins, odor in identifying, 23
Trauma, causes of death from, 165-166
Triage, 18
Tuberculosis, 177-178

V

Vaso-vagal reaction and sudden death, 22, 186
Vegetative state in dying, 6-7
Ventilator, 37
Ventricular fibrillation, 5, 169
Ventricular tachycardia, 169
Viral encephalitis, 181-182
Vital signs, 19
Voodoo, 186-187

W

Worked to death, 171-172

X

X Ray in autopsy, 73, 75, 78

Y

"Y" incision in autopsy, 79, 80, 83-84